ENAMS

ENERGY OPTIMIZATION ALGORITHM FOR MOBILE WIRELESS SENSOR NETWORKS

ENAMS
ENERGY OPTIMIZATION ALGORITHM FOR MOBILE WIRELESS SENSOR NETWORKS

C B DASS
NIPUN DAS

KNOWLEDGE
BAKERS

KNOWLEDGE BAKERS

Cataloging in Publication Data--DK

Courtesy: D.K. Agencies (P) Ltd. <docinfo@dkagencies.com>

Dass, C. B., author.

ENAMS : energy optimization algorithm for mobile wireless sensor networks / by CB Dass & Nipun Das.

pages cm

Includes bibliographical references.

ISBN 9789391502539

1. Wireless Sensor Networks. 2. Swarm intelligence. I. Title.

LCC TK7872.D48D37 2023 | DDC 006.25 23

ISBN: 978-93-91502-53-9

9 789391 502539

Published by : **Knowledge Bakers**
Pune, India
Email: knowledgebakers2019@gmail.com

Digitally Printed at : **Replika Press Pvt. Ltd.**

ACKNOWLEDGEMENTS

I would like to express my sincere appreciation and gratitude to ***Dr. Aladdin Ayesh*** for his supervision, guidance and support throughout my Ph.D. study. Meetings with him were enjoyable and discussions were insightful. The only thing I can say to him is thank you for everything.

Also, I would like to thank *Prof. Alaa Sheta* for being a very nice advisor and brother during my first period being in De Montfort University.

Deep appreciation and thanks to my dearest wife for her endurance to put up with my hectic life style for being a Ph.D. student. She kept me happy and sane during the Ph.D. process, and I thank her for all her patience and her never-ending optimism when I came home late, frustrated, and stressed.

I would like to thank all my colleagues at De Montfort University. Special appreciation goes to *Dr. Ali Al-Bayatti* for his significant cooperation and support making the Ph.D. period such a friendly environment.

I would like to thank my family, all my sisters and brothers for all their love and support. I am very lucky to have such wonderful family members.

At last, I want to dedicate my thesis to my father and beloved mother who passed away few years ago.

CB Dass

CONTENTS

Page

LIST OF FIGURES

Page

List of Acronyms

ACM	Access Control Mechanism
ACO	Ant Colony Optimization
ADC	Analog to Digital Converter
CH	Cluster Head
CMOS	Complementary Metal Oxide Semiconductor
CPU	Central Processing Unit
DARPA	Defence Advanced Research Project Agency
DC	Data Collector
DNS	Domain Name Service
EAs	Evolutionary Algorithms
ESB	Embedded Sensor Board
GAs	Genetic Algorithms
GPS	Global Positioning System
IR	Infrared
ITS	Intelligent Transportation Systems
MAC	Medium Access Control
MANET	Mobile Ad hoc Network
NS-2	Network Simulator-2
PC	Personal computer
PSO	Particle Swarm Optimization
QoS	Quality of Service
RF	Radio Frequency
RFID	Radio Frequency Identification
RSSI	Received Signal Strength Indicator
SI	Swarm Intelligence

TSP	Travelling Salesman Problem
WLAN	Wireless Local Area Network
WSN	Wireless sensor Network
XML	Extensible Markup Language

Chapter 1

Introduction

1.1 Introduction

Recent advances in micro-electro-mechanical systems, digital electronics, and wireless communications have led to the emergence of wireless sensor networks (WSNs), which consist of a large number of sensing devices each capable of detecting, processing, and transmitting environmental information. A single sensor node may only be equipped with limited computation and communication capabilities; however, nodes in a WSN, when properly configured, can collaboratively perform signal processing tasks to obtain information of a remote and probably a dangerous area in an untended and robust way. Applications of wireless sensors networks include battlefield surveillance, environmental monitoring, biological detection, smart spaces, industrial diagnostics, etc. [7]. Figure 1.1 depicts a typical application of WSNs: target detection, tracking, and classification [80, 154].

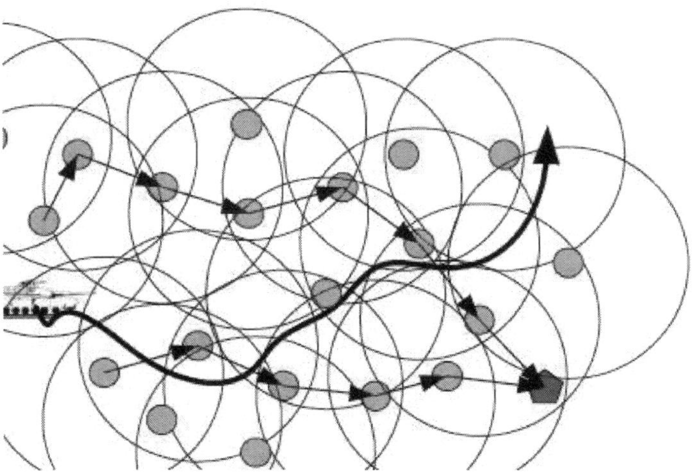

Figure 1.1: Sensor nodes send their measurements to the sink (fusion centre) via wireless multi-hop communications. The circles around the

sensors represents the radio range of each node.

In this application scenario, the information processing tasks are to let the sink-point (data collector) infer, based on the collected information from the deployed sensor nodes, what type the target is and where the target is. To accomplish these information processing tasks, a naive approach is to let nodes send their measurements (e.g., an acoustic sensor measures the amplitude of the received sound signal) to the sink, possibly via multi-hop communications as shown in Fig. 1.1, and let the sink process the measurements. However, this approach is not energy efficient. It has been widely argued that the transmission and reception energy per bit is much larger than sensing and processing energy per bit [53, 140]. In general, the raw data of a node's measurements is of large volume. Transmitting raw measured data not only consumes large amount of energy but also increases network traffic which poses high bandwidth demand.

Energy efficiency has been deemed as the main challenge in the Wireless Sensor Networks. Generally, the power supply of a single sensor node relies on a battery with limited energy (e.g., an AAA battery). Changing or recharging nodes' battery is very difficult, if not impossible, after sensor nodes have been deployed. Therefore, it is desirable to design energy efficient protocols to run on individual nodes such that the operation time of the deployed WSN can be maintained as long as possible. Some classical information processing approaches, however, do not consider the energy efficiency issue and need to be re-examined when applied in resource constrained WSNs. Geographically distributed nodes in a WSN may have different views of the physical phenomenon in the sensor field and their measurements may have some correlations. A well-designed algorithm should also exploit this to accomplish the information processing task via collaboration among nodes.

1.2 Motivation

Wireless communication technologies are undergoing rapid advancements. The last few years have experienced a steep growth in research in the area of wireless sensor networks (WSNs). In WSNs, communication takes place with the help of spatially distributed autonomous sensor nodes equipped to sense specific information.

WSNs, especially the ones that have gained much popularity in the recent years, are typically, ad hoc in nature and they inherit many characteristics/features of wireless ad hoc networks such as the ability for infrastructure-less setup, minimal or no reliance on network planning, and the ability of the nodes to self-organize and self-configure without the involvement of a centralized network manager, router, access point, or a switch. These features help to setup WSNs fast in situations where there is no existing network setup or in times when setting up a fixed infrastructure network is considered infeasible, for example, in times of emergency or during relief operations. WSNs have variety of applications in both the military and the civilian population worldwide such as in cases of enemy intrusion in the battlefield object tracking, habitat monitoring, patient monitoring, fire detection, and so on.

Even though sensor networks have emerged to be attractive and they hold great promises for our future, there are several challenges that need to be addressed. Some of the well-known challenges are attributed to issues relating to coverage and deployment, scalability, quality-of-service, size, computational power, energy efficiency, and security.

With the rapid development in miniaturization, low power wireless communication, micro-sensor, and microprocessor hardware, it have become a reality to deploy small, inexpensive, low-power, distributed devices, which are capable of monitoring physical environment by local processing and wireless communication.

As the Internet has revolutionized our life by the exchange of various forms of information among a large number of users, WSNs may, in the near future, be equally significant by providing information of the physical phenomena of interest and ultimately being able to detect and control them or enable us to construct more accurate models of the physical world.

Generally, when people consider wireless devices they think of items such as cell phones, personal digital assistants, or laptops with 802.11 standards. These items costs hundreds of dollars, target specialised applications, and rely on the pre-deployment of extensive infrastructure support. In contrast, Wireless Sensor Networks use small, low-cost embedded devices for a wide range of applications and do not rely on any pre-existing infrastructure.

While it is important to provide timely delivery of data for most applications, an efficient use of the mobile sensor-network's limited energy resource must also be considered. Sensor nodes typically operate on batteries and have finite energy, but in many applications, the network is expected to have a long operating lifetime. Compared to sensing and data processing, data communication and sensor's mobility are typically incurs the highest energy consumption.

1.3 Research Aims

The main aim of this research is to minimise the energy consumption in mobile Wireless Sensor Networks by optimising the communication distance between the sensor-nodes and the data collector (sink-point). To achieve this aim, we need to design an algorithm that will divide the sensor-nodes into clusters and enables these clusters to keep the optimised topology while they are directed to achieve a given goal. This algorithm should be fast, randomized, and distributed algorithm for organising the sensors in a mobile Wireless Sensor Network with an objective of minimising the energy spent in communicating the information to the data collector. The target networks are those consist of large scale, heavily constrained embedded devices suitable for industrial, military and commercial applications.

Many clustering algorithms in various contexts have been proposed in the past [143, 144, 148, 156]. These are dicussed in details in Chapter 2. These algorithms are mostly heuristic in nature and aim at generating the minimum number of clusters in static networks with distance optimisation of around 75%. In this research we are aiming to expand this optimisation problem to be applied for both static and mobile Wireless Sensor Networks and to achieve distance optimisation of around 80% as compared with the distance of direct transmission. The design of the proposed algorithm is based on Evolutionary Computation and Swarm Intelligence. In the first phase of the algorithm, Genetic Algorithms (GAs) to be used for clustering the sensor-nodes into independent clusters to minimize the overall communication distance for the sensor network. One of challenging assumptions for the presented algorithm is that the number of clusters within the sensor network is not necessary to be predefined. This gives more flexibility for the node deployment process in the sensor network. Another assumption is that, the density of the sensors in each cluster not necessary to be uniform for all the clusters as in most previous clustering algorithms. This will support the application constraints for different kinds of Wireless Sensor Networks, where the sensors need to be deployed in different densities depending on the nature of the location where the sensor-nodes to be deployed.

The second phase of the algorithm is based on Particle Swarms Optimisation (PSO) to keep the optimum distribution of the sensor-nodes and to eliminate any unnecessary movements for mobile sensors while they are directed as a swarm to achieve a given goal.

1.4 Research Methodology

A key component to the design of an optimisation algorithm is a thorough knowledge and understanding of the factors that influence the specific Wireless Sensor Networks (WSNs) for which the algorithm is intended.

To achieve the goals of the proposed algorithm mentioned in the previous section, the research is divided into three distinct phases.

The first phase involved a thorough literature review where the related work was studied to investigate the factors that influence the design of an energy optimisation algorithm to enlarge the life time of mobile Wireless Sensor Networks. The literature study also includes an investigation into the available optimisation algorithms and protocols which are related to Wireless Sensor Networks in order to identify the common problems faced by these algorithms.

The second phase involved the design and implementation of the proposed algorithm starting with static sensor-nodes as a first stage, in which the positions of sensor nodes are assumed to be fixed. In the second stage of phase two, more challenging WSNs were considered which are networks having mobile wireless sensor nodes. To allow the rapid evaluation and adjustment of the proposed algorithm, a simulation system was implemented in this phase by using Java programming language to verify the goals of the presented algorithm.

The third phase was dedicated to the hardware experimentation using mobile Robots to verify the objectives of the presented algorithm and proving its portability from the simulation environment to physical swarm of mobile sensors. Finally, result analysis and critical review was achieved.

1.5 Thesis Outline

The rest of this thesis is structured as follows:

Chapter-2: presents a general overview of WSNs and how it differs from other traditional wireless networks. A wide range of WSN applications also presented in this chapter. The major challenges and hardware constraints are explained in this chapter. The clustered topology as a solution for minimizing the energy dissipation in the WSNs is outlined within this Chapter.

Chapter-3: demonstrates the swarm intelligence (SI) concepts and how it can be used as a computational and behavioural metaphor for solving distributed and complex problems. The main concentration in this chapter is devoted to explain Particle Swarm Optimization (PSO) and Evolutionary Algorithms, specifically Genetic Algorithms (GAs) as optimization techniques that the proposed system in this thesis is based on Finally, the previous work and achievements which have been done in this field are demonstrated.

Chapter-4: presents the new algorithm ENAMS, which is mainly consists of two stages. In the first stage, the distance optimization for WSNs is achieved by using GAs to divide the sensor nodes into K-independent clusters. In the second stage, the distance management for the mobile Ad Hoc WSNs depending on Particle Swarm Optimization (PSO) is demonstrated.

Chapter-5: presents the software implementation of ENAMS algorithm, by showing the evolved clustered topology of the WSN and then how are those clusters will be directed as swarms keeping the optimum deployment of the sensor nodes to achieve a given goal.

Chapter-6: shows the implementation of ENAMS algorithm in a real world environment by using swarmed mobile robots of type NXT-Mindstorms to prove the portability of our algorithm from the simulation environment into a physical platform.

Chapter-7: summarizes the presented work of this thesis and highlights the significance of the contributions made with an analytical observations. This chapter is ended by discussing the directions for future work.

Chapter 2

Wireless Sensor Networks (WSNs)

2.1 Introduction

A Wireless Sensor Network (WSN) consists of sensor nodes connected among themselves by a wireless medium to perform distributed sensing tasks. This type of networks are expected to be used in different applications such as environmental and health monitoring, surveillance, and security [78, 4]. Sensor networks are a sensing, computing and communication infrastructure that allows us to instrument, observe, and respond to phenomena in the natural environment, and in our physical and cyber infrastructure. The sensors themselves can range from small passive microsensors (e.g., "smart dust") to larger scale, controllable weather-sensing platforms. Their computation and communication infrastructure will be radically different from that found in today's Internet-based systems, reflecting the device and application driven nature of these systems. An important aspect of WSNs comes from having many sensors generating sensing data for the same set of events.

2.1.1 WSNs verses Traditional Wireless Networks

Although many protocols and algorithms have been proposed for traditional wireless ad hoc networks, they are not well suited to the unique features and application requirements of sensor networks [150]. Sensor networks is a new family of wireless networks and is significantly differs from traditional networks like cellular networks and MANETs. In such traditional networks, the tasks organization, routing and mobility management is done to optimize the Quality of Service (QoS) and high bandwidth efficiency [119]. These networks are designed to provide good throughput/delay characteristics under high mobility conditions. Energy consumption is of secondary importance as the battery packs can be replaced as needed.

However, sensor networks consist of hundreds to thousands of nodes that are designed for unattended operation. The traffic is of a statistical nature as compared to the multimedia rich data in MANETs and cellular networks. The data rate is expected to be very low to the order of 1-100 kb/

sec. unlike conventional networks, the main goals are prolonging the life of the network and prevent connectivity degradation through aggressive energy management as the batteries cannot usually be replaced because of operations in hostile or remote environments. In sensor networks the flow of data is predominantly unidirectional from the sensor nodes to the sink-point.

The following points illustrates some features of WSNs which make it different to other traditional networks [7, 4]:

- The number of sensor nodes in a wireless sensor network can be several orders of magnitude higher than the nodes in other wireless networks.
- Sensor nodes are densely deployed.
- Sensor nodes are prone to failures.
- The topology of a sensor network changes very frequently.
- Sensor nodes mainly use a broadcast communication paradigm, whereas most ad hoc networks are based on point-to-point communications.
- Sensor nodes are limited in power, computational capacities, and memory.
- Sensor nodes may not have global identification (ID) because of the large amount of overhead and large number of sensors.

2.1.2 Types of Sensor Networks

Current WSNs are deployed on land, underground, and underwater. Depending on the environment, a sensor network faces different challenges and constraints. There are five types of WSNs: terrestrial WSN, underground WSN, underwater WSN, multi-media WSN, and mobile WSN.

Terrestrial WSNs [7] typically consist of hundreds to thousands of inexpensive wireless sensor nodes deployed in a given area, either in an ad hoc or in a pre-planned manner. In ad hoc deployment, sensor nodes can be dropped from a plane and randomly placed into the target area. In pre-planned deployment, there is grid placement, optimal placement [130], 2-d and 3-d placement models [149, 105].

In a terrestrial WSN, reliable communication in a dense environment is very important. Terrestrial sensor nodes must be able to effectively communicate data back to the base station. While battery power is limited and may not be rechargeable, terrestrial sensor nodes however can be equipped with a secondary power source such as solar cells. In any case, it is important for sensor nodes to conserve energy. For a terrestrial WSN, energy can be conserved with multi-hop optimal routing, short transmission range, in-network data aggregation, eliminating data redundancy, minimizing delays, and using low duty-cycle operations.

Underground WSNs [6, 81] consist of a number of sensor nodes buried under-ground or in a cave or mine used to monitor underground conditions. Additional sink nodes are located above ground to relay information from the sensor nodes to the base station. An underground WSN is more expensive than a terrestrial WSN in terms of equipment, deployment, and maintenance. Underground sensor nodes are expensive because appropriate equipment parts must be selected to ensure reliable communication through soil, rocks, water, and other mineral contents. The underground environment makes wireless communication a challenge due to signal losses and high levels of attenuation. Unlike terrestrial WSNs, the deployment of an underground WSN requires careful planning and energy and cost considerations. Energy is an important concern in underground WSNs. Like terrestrial WSN, underground sensor nodes are equipped with a limited battery power and once deployed into the ground, it is difficult to recharge or replace a sensor node's battery. As before, a key objective is to conserve energy in order to increase the lifetime of network which can be achieved by implementing efficient communication protocol.

Underwater WSNs [5, 51] consist of a number of sensor nodes and vehicles deployed underwater. As opposite to terrestrial WSNs, underwater sensor nodes are more expensive and fewer sensor nodes are deployed. Autonomous underwater vehicles are used for exploration or gathering data from sensor nodes. Compared to a dense deployment of sensor nodes in a terrestrial WSN, a sparse deployment of sensor nodes is placed underwater. Typical underwater wireless communications are established through transmission of acoustic waves. A challenge in underwater acoustic communication is the limited bandwidth, long propagation delay, and signal fading issues. Another challenge is sensor node failure due to environmental conditions. Underwater sensor nodes must be able to self-configure and adapt to harsh ocean environment. Underwater sensor nodes are equipped with a limited battery which cannot be replaced or recharged. The issue of energy conservation for underwater WSNs involves developing efficient underwater communication and networking techniques.

Multi-media WSNs [4] have been proposed to enable monitoring and tracking of events in the form of multimedia such as video, audio, and imaging. Multi-media WSNs consist of a number of low cost sensor nodes equipped with cameras and microphones. These sensor nodes interconnect with each other over a wireless connection for data retrieval, process, correlation, and compression. Multi-media sensor nodes are deployed in a pre-planned manner into the environment to guarantee coverage. Challenges in multi-media WSN include high bandwidth demand, high energy consumption, quality of service (QoS) provisioning, data processing and compressing techniques, and cross-layer design. Multi-media content such as a video stream requires high bandwidth in order for the content to be delivered. As a result, high data rate leads to high energy consumption. Transmission techniques that support high bandwidth and low energy consumption have to be developed. QoS provisioning is a challenging task in a multi-media WSN due to the variable delay and variable channel capacity. It is important that a certain level of QoS must be achieved for reliable content delivery. In-network processing, filtering and compression can significantly improve network performance in terms of filtering and extracting redundant information and merging contents. Similarly, cross-layer interaction among the layers can improve the processing and the delivery process.

Mobile WSNs [151, 144, 148, 128, 115] consist of a collection of sensor nodes that can move on their own and interact with the physical environment. Mobile nodes have the ability to sense, compute, and communicate like static nodes. A key difference is mobile nodes have the ability to reposition and organize itself in the network. A mobile WSN can start off with some initial deployment and nodes can then spread out to gather information. Information gathered by a mobile node can be communicated to another mobile node when they are within range of each other. Another key difference is data distribution. In a static WSN, data can be distributed using fixed routing or flooding while dynamic routing is used in a mobile WSN. Challenges in mobile WSN include deployment, localization, self-organization, navigation and control, coverage, energy, maintenance, and data process.

Mobile WSN applications are included but not limited to environment monitoring, target tracking, search and rescue, and real-time monitoring of hazardous material. For environmental monitoring in disaster areas, manual deployment might not be possible. With mobile sensor nodes, they can move to areas of events after deployment to provide the required coverage. In military surveillance and tracking, mobile sensor nodes can collaborate and make decisions based on the target. Mobile sensor nodes can achieve a higher degree of coverage and connectivity compared to static sensor nodes. In the presence of obstacles in the field, mobile sensor nodes can plan ahead and move appropriately to obstructed regions to increase target exposure.

2.1.3 Hardware Constraints of Sensors

A sensor is a physical device that probes physical, biological, or chemical properties of its environment and converts these properties into an electrical signal. Sensors for temperature, light, oxygen, distance, blood pressure, moisture, and torque are some of the many examples, Figure 2.1 shows some examples for sensors platforms [78].

Figure 2.1: Examples of Sensor Platforms [80]

An actuator typically accepts an electrical signal and converts it into a physical action to act upon the environment. Sensors and actuators belong to the broader family of transducers. Classical transducers such as temperature or pressure sensors are available as off-the-shelf components and can be easily integrated at the board or package level. More complex ones like CMOS image sensors, inertial sensors, or micro-fluidic actuators have recently emerged [56], thanks to technological advances. Those "smart" sensors typically require dedicated logic for calibration, signal processing, or analog-to-digital conversion and sometimes include a micro-controller [78].

A sensor node is made up of four basic components, as shown in Figure 2.2: a sensing unit, a processing unit, a transceiver unit, and a power unit. They may also have additional application-dependent components such as a location finding system, power generator, and mobilizer.

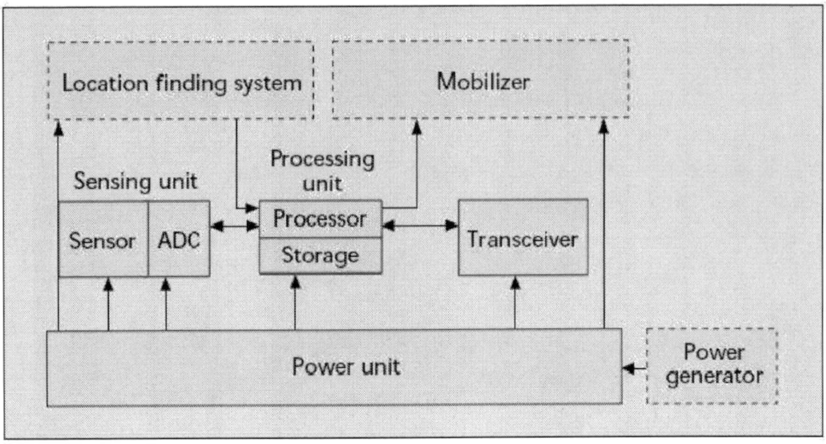

Figure 2.2: Block diagram of the main components in a sensor node [80]

Sensing units are usually composed of two subunits: sensors and analog-to-digital converters (ADCs). The analog signals produced by the sensors based on the observed phenomenon are converted to digital signals by the ADC, and then fed into the processing unit. The processing unit, which is generally associated with a small storage unit, manages the procedures that make the sensor node collab-orate with the other nodes to carry out the assigned sensing tasks. A transceiver unit connects the node to the network.

One of the most important components of a sensor node is the power unit. Power units may be supported by power scavenging units such as solar cells. There are also other subunits that are application-dependent. Figure 2.3 shows an image of the Embedded Sensor Board (ESB) developed by the FU-Berlin company.

Most of the sensor network routing techniques and sensing tasks require knowledge of location with high accuracy. Thus, it is common that a sensor node has a location finding system. A mobilizer may sometimes be needed to move sensor nodes when it is required to carry out the assigned tasks. All of these subunits may need to fit into a matchbox-sized module [62]. The required size may be smaller than even a cubic centimetre, which is light enough to remain suspended in the air [106]. Apart from size, there is some other stringent constraints for sensor nodes. These nodes must consume at an extremely low power, operate in high volumetric densities, have low production cost, be dispensable and autonomous, operate unattended, and be adaptive to the environment.

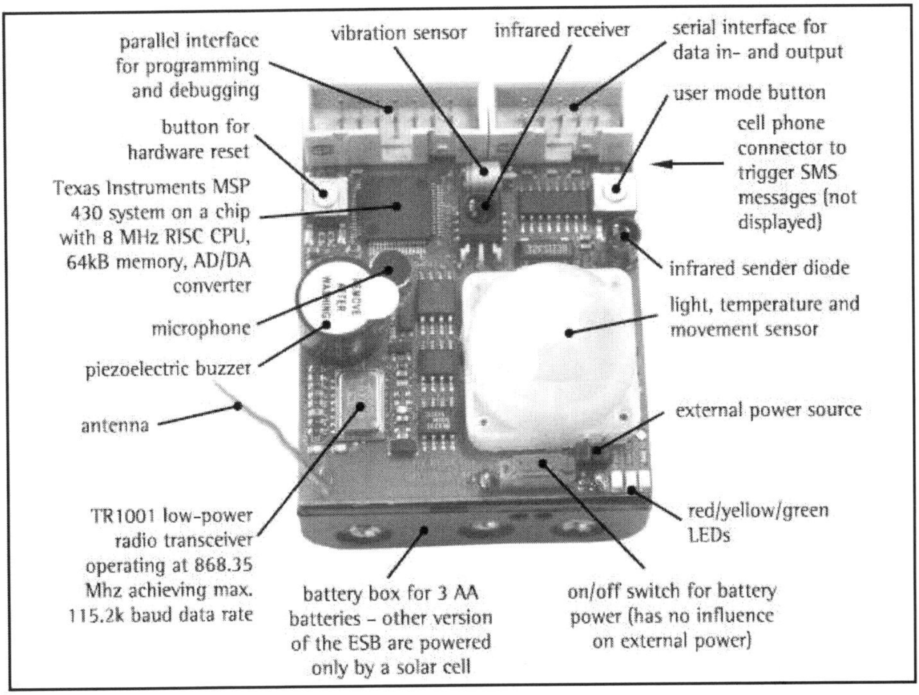

Figure 2.3: Embedded Sensor Board (ESB) components from the FU-Berlin [64]

2.1.4 Challenges in Ad Hoc WSNs

This section shows the major challenges that the design and operation of Ad Hoc WSNs face which mainly comes from the lack of infrastructure. The major issues and challenges that affect the design, performance and operation of such types of networks are listed below [4, 5, 128, 25, 69, 155]:

- Routing
- Energy Efficiency
- Self-Organization
- Medium Access Scheme
- Security
- Scalability
- Quality of Service Provisioning
- Deployment Considerations
- Multicasting

- Addressing and Service Discovery

All of the envisaged applications require cheap sensors networks. The wireless sensor nodes themselves must cost very little, and this means that the devices must have a small silicon area to reduce their cost. Of course, this small die area means that memory and digital computational circuitry will be limited. This constraint places a burden on the chip designer implementing security on the device, as approaches that consume a lot of die area cannot be entertained.

In some of application areas of WSN it will not be possible, for reasons of cost or accessibility, to replace the power source when it is depleted. Conserving energy is vital for the network to operate as long as possible. The radio will be the main source of power dissipation in the device, and so should operate with a low duty cycle - less than 1. It has been found that in a state of the art radio, the energy required to transmit one bit can be dominated by the start-up energy. This is because the packets to be transmitted are typically very small in wireless sensor networks. The transceiver should be designed so that the start-up time before the data can be transmitted or received is as small as possible [116]. The digital circuitry should be designed with the aim of reducing the energy consumption using well-known techniques.

It is also important that establishing the network is not an expensive process. It should be possible for a person who is not an engineer to deploy these networks. Therefore the WSN has to be self-configuring, and robust to individual device failure. Of course, the application programming of the wireless sensor nodes would have been carried out by an engineer but the end user should just be able to scatter the wireless sensor nodes and expect them to autonomously establish a viable WSN.

A measurement taken from a wireless sensor node consists of three main components; the physical measurement, the time it was taken and the position of the device. Synchronization of the devices will be required to get a valid time stamp for the reading. This can be achieved by the broadcasting of synchronization packets from a wireless sensor node within a WSN as there may only be occasional interaction with the gateway device that injects or extracts data from the WSN. The end users of the system will not be concerned with a reading from an individual node but rather with the position from which the reading originated. Therefore it is also required that the wireless sensor nodes know their position, at least relative to one another, and this is a challenging problem.

Most of the applications outlined in this thesis (see Section 2.2) require some level of security: the driver who is speeding will not want this information to become public; the company that is measuring the pollution that they are creating in the environment will wish to release that information in a controlled way; the patient in the hospital will want to be sure that his private medical records remain private. So, in order for these networks to be deployed in most applications, it is essential that the issue of security is solved, as noted in [102, 25].

Our consideration for this research will be focused on the *Energy Efficiency* as it is one of the vital challenges in the Mobile Ad Hoc WSNs.

2.1.5 Energy-Aware Wireless Sensor Networks

Nodes in a WSN are usually highly energy-constrained and expected to operate for long periods from limited on-board energy reserves. To permit this, nodes and the embedded software that they execute must have energy-aware operation. Energy efficiency has been of significant importance since WSNs were first conceived but, as certain applications have emerged and evolved [65], a real need for ultra-miniaturized long-life devices has re-emerged as a dominant requirement. Because of this, continued developments in energy-efficient operation are paramount, requiring major advances to be made in energy hardware, power management circuitry and energy-aware algorithms and protocols.

The energy components of a typical wireless sensor node are shown in Figure 2.4. Energy is provided to the node from an energy source, whether this is a form of energy harvesting from sources such as solar, vibration or wind, or a resource such as the mains supply or the manual provision and replacement of primary batteries. Energy obtained from the energy source is buff in an energy store; this is usually a battery or super capacitor. Finally, energy is used by the node's energy consumers; these are hardware components such as; the microcontroller, radio transceiver, sensors and peripherals.

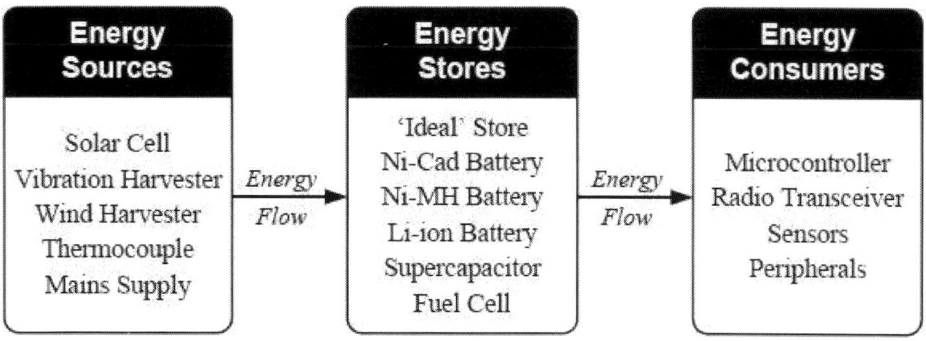

Figure 2.4: Energy components of a typical sensor node

With the increased usage of energy sources in nodes [100, 129], the need for energy stores other than batteries (many of which suffer from only offering a limited number of charging cycles) is increased. This can be seen by the researchs that are now utilizing super capacitors (devices that are similar to standard electrolytic capacitors, but with capacities of many Farads) to store the node's energy [129, 64].

To be energy-aware, the embedded software executing on the node must be aware of the state of its energy components. This may be as advanced as monitoring the energy harvested from each source [142], inspecting the rate of consumption by different consumers [120], directing the flow of energy from and to different stores and managing the charging of rechargeable stores [64]. Alternatively, this may equate to simply being able to inspect the residual energy in a single store. Therefore, the embedded software must not only be capable of interfacing with energy hardware (this is generally a requirement of power management circuitry), but also interpreting the data that are obtained usually in the form of a sampled voltage into a remaining lifetime, power or energy. Based upon these values, the operation of the node is adjusted accordingly, usually to maximize the lifetime of the network.

2.2 Applications of Ad Hoc WSNs

Due to the fast and less demanding deployment of ad hoc sensor networks, we can find this type of networks in several areas. Some of these areas includes: military applications (search and rescue missions), multi-user games, robotics pets, collaborative and distributive computing, emergency operations, wireless mesh networks. In health, sensor nodes can also be deployed to monitor patients and assist disabled patients. Some other commercial applications include managing inventory, monitoring product quality, and monitoring disaster areas [92]. Generally, WSN applications can be classified into two categories [150]: monitoring and tracking (see Figure 2.5).

Monitoring applications include indoor/outdoor environmental monitoring, health and wellness monitoring, power monitoring, inventory location monitoring, factory and process automation, and seismic and structural monitoring. Tracking applications include tracking objects, animals, humans, and vehicles. Some of the main application areas for Ad Hoc wireless sensors networks are described in the following sections.

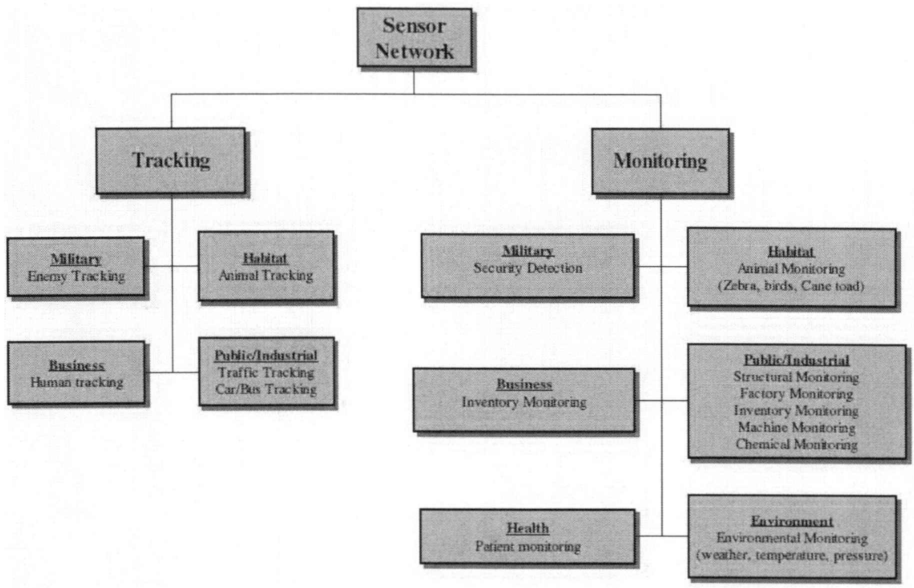

Figure 2.5: Overview of Sensor Networks applications [154]

2.2.1 Intelligent Transportation Systems

Intelligent Transportation Systems (ITS) is the application of sensing, communication and control technologies to the road transportation system, with the aim of reducing congestion or improving road user's safety. It is a field in which wireless sensor networks could make a valuable contribution [30, 29].

The use of wireless sensor networks in ITS will enable much more data and different types of data to be incorporated into traffic management systems. There is also a need for security in the traffic enforcement scenario and also in the general case of information from wireless sensor nodes being able to contribute to the changing of traffic signals.

2.2.2 Healthcare

There are several projects in the application of wireless sensor nodes to the area of patient healthcare in emergency medicine [49, 42]. When the paramedics and doctors arrive at mass casualty incident they have to classify the injured into critical (red), urgent (yellow) and minor (green). Following this initial classification they have to monitor the different patients to ensure that their condition does not deteriorate. If there are a lot of patients and not very many medical personnel this process would be time consuming and lead to the doctor having to stop treating a particular patient to check the vital signs of another patient. John Hopkins University have designed a system, which uses the Mica-Z mote from Crossbow Technology to assist in this process [89].

2.2.3 Environmental Monitoring

Sensors can play an important role in environmental threat detection. Chemical sensors attached to devices with integrated Radio Frequency (RF) transceivers can provide an early warning system to rescuers. They provide information on the toxic gas present and also the position of the contaminant.

Some environmental applications of sensor networks include monitoring environmental conditions are listed below:

- Forest firedetection [26]
- Flood detection [20, 2, 61]
- Biocomplexity mapping of the environment [24, 33, 136]
- Precision Agriculture [9]

2.2.4 Military Applications

Incorporating wireless sensor networks in the military applications can play an integral part of military command, control, communications, computing, intelligence, surveillance, reconnaissance and targeting (C4ISRT) systems [144, 1]. The rapid deployment, self-organization and fault tolerance characteristics of sensor networks make them a very promising sensing technique for military C4ISRT. Since the design of sensor networks is based on the dense deployment of disposable and low-cost sensor nodes, destruction of some nodes by hostile actions does not affect a military operation as much as the destruction of a traditional sensor, this makes sensor networks concept a better solution for battlefields [124].

2.2.5 Home Automation

With the advanced in the electronic and memory technologies, smart sensor nodes and actuators can be embedded in appliances, such as; micro-wave ovens, vacuum cleaners, refrigerators, and VCRs [103]. The sensors in such devices can interact with each other and with the external network via the Internet or Satellite communications. They allow end users to manage home devices locally as well as remotely with an easier manner.

2.3 Existing Simulators for Wireless Networks

Analysing networks is usually done by using one of the following three techniques: (1) analytical methods, (2) computer simulations, and (3) practical implementations [108]. The constraints and complexity of WSNs often cause analytical methods to be unsuitable or inaccurate [28]. Additionally, the proportion of algorithms that are analysed through practical evaluation is comparatively low, possibly due to the relative infancy, deployment cost, broad diversity, and application dependence of WSNs. As a result, simulation is currently the most widely adopted method of analysing WSNs, allowing the rapid evaluation, optimisation, and adjustment of proposed algorithms and protocols. Simulation allows certain areas of network operation to be left out or simplified; for example assuming that packet collisions, interference and noise do not occur, that nodes are always perfectly synchronised with one another, or that particular consumers do not consume any energy. These simplifications often make the process of development and evaluation faster and easier, but can result in algorithms that are not realisable in practice; hence a simulation is only as realistic as the models and assumptions that it is based upon.

While simulation is reasonably well established for Mobile Ad Hoc Networks (MANETs), the simulation of WSNs not only requires the implementation of a radio channel, but also a physical environment and accurate energy models. The design aims and strategies of different simulators result in them each having different strengths and weaknesses; an appreciation of this is essential in either selecting a simulator, or simulation creation. Simulators for use with WSNs can be classified into two predominant categories: those that have been developed as extensions to existing network simulators (such as the SensorSim [101] extension to NS-2 [94], and those that have been designed specifically for the WSNs simulation (such as J-Sim [118]).

In the following, we provide an overview of the design and architecture of some of the major WSN simulators:

NS-2 [94] probably the most popular simulation tool for sensor networks, which is an object-orientated discrete event network simulator based upon the real network simulator (NS) that was released in 1989. It is reportedly hard to make changes to and develop extensions for [28]. While this is not such a problem for traditional networks (protocols such as Ethernet and TCP do not require alterations as they are well established), it poses obstacles in the simulation of WSNs. Though NS-2 is relatively complicated to use, researchers are often happy to invest their time in learning how to use it due to its popularity and user-base. The extensibility of NS-2 has been a major contributor to its success, with protocol implementations being widely produced and developed by the research community. Additionally however, NS-2 is limited by its scalability (interdependencies between objects in the object-orientated design do not scale well) and the lack of an application model (sensor networks often require interactions between network and application layers).

SensorSim [101] is an extension of NS-2 aimed at the simulation of WSNs. SensorSim provides advanced models and the ability to interact with external applications (such as real sensor network hardware). SensorSim is currently withdrawn from release and, as it is built on top of NS-2, suffers from the same scalability problems.

Like NS-2, **OMNeT++** [133] is a discrete-event general purpose network simulator. OMNeT++ is structured around a modular system: simple modules (such as layers of a protocol stack) contain algorithms, making up the lowest level of hierarchy, while compound modules (such as a sensor node) contain simple modules that interact with each other using messages. OMNeT++ has a versatile Graphical User Interface (GUI) allowing, for example, the user to inspect interconnections between modules and the messages being transferred between them.

SenSim [134] is a sensor network extension for OMNeT++. Within the complex module of a node, modules are present to represent each protocol layer, the hardware, and a coordinator (responsible for passing messages around the node). Additional modules outside of the nodes represent a sensor channel and a network channel. However, use of SenSim requires a reasonably high learning curve, which is generally not popular with simulators that are not widely established. Also, due to the lack of a significant user base, there are not many developed protocols available for it.

Castalia [93] simulator is also built upon OMNeT++, and is a model-centric extension for WSNs, providing a range of accurate models to the end-user.

The **GTSNetS** simulator [99] is a sensor network extension to the GTNetS simulator, which aims to provide a scalable, highly extensible and customisable, model-centric simulator to WSN researchers, and also enables the simulation of sensor control networks.

OPNET [48] is an object-orientated network simulator, originally it was developed for the needs of military, but it has grown to be a world leading commercial network simulation tool. It enables the possibility to simulate entire heterogeneous networks with various protocols. The software of this simulator is built on top of a discrete event system. It simulates the system behavior by modeling each event happening in the system and processes it by user-defined processes. It uses a hierarchical strategy to organize all the models to build a whole network [98]. The hierarchy models entities from physical link transceivers, antennas, to CPU running processes to manage queues or running protocols, to devices modelled by nodes with process modules and transceivers, to network model that connects all different kinds of nodes together. OPNET is quite expensive for commercial usage but there are also free licenses for educational purposes. It consists of high level user interface, which is constructed from C and C++ source code blocks with a huge library of OPNET specific functions. However, due to scalability and extensibility issues, it is not widely used for WSN simulation.

J-Sim [118] is designed around a component structure in order to overcome scalability issues inherent in object-orientated structures. While its component-oriented structure increases its scalability, the implementation choice of Java (which makes it truly crossplatform) arguably reduces the possible efficiency of the simulator.

J-Sim is relatively complicated to use and, due to no real established user base, is not widely adopted.

SENSE (Sensor Network Simulator and Emulator) [28] improves on the efficiency of J-SIM by providing a component-orientated architecture programmed in C++, and improving on the inter-communication efficiency of J-Sim. However, SENSE lacks developed extensibility, and does not include functionality such as sensing.

TOSSIM [79] is both a simulator and an emulator for WSNs, in that it simulates TinyOS code for the Mica range of nodes. All nodes in the network must run identical code and, while sensor hardware is modelled, the environment is not. However, TOSSIM provides obvious advantages to projects that are to be implemented on the MICA nodes.

Table 2.1 summarise the main features and limitations that could be found for all the simulators explained in this section.

2.4 Clustered Topology for WSNs

Cluster analysis or *clustering* is the assignment of a set of observations into subsets (called clusters) so that observations in the same cluster are similar in some sense [43]. Clustering is a method of unsupervised learning, and a common technique for statistical data analysis used in many fields including machine learning, data mining, pattern recognition, image analysis and bioinformatics.

Among many challenges faced by ad-hoc and sensor networks designers, *scalability* is a critical issue. The flat topology of these types of networks contains a large number of nodes that have to compete for the limited wireless band-width, handle sizable routing tables and manage substantial traffic caused by network dynamics. One promising approach to solve the scalability problem is to abstract the network topology by building hierarchies of nodes. This process is commonly referred to as *clustering*.

Table 2.1: A Comparison of Existing Network Simulators

Simulator	Main Features	Limitations
NS-2	Object oriented discrete event Popular	Not easy to use; Hard to make changed; Hard to develop extensions; Lack of Application Layer model; Limited in Scalability
SensorSim	Object oriented discrete event; Provides advanced models for network hardware	Hard to develop extensions; Limited in Scalability
OMNeT++	Discrete-event; Structured around simple modules; Has a versatile GUI	Model building may require special training; Needs long time for learning how to use the simulation packages; Results may be difficult to interpret
SenSim	Modules are present to represent each protocol layer	Requires a reasonably high learning; There are not many developed protocols available for it
Castalia	Built upon OMNeT++ simulator; Provides a range of accurate models to the end-user	Users needs to build their custom routing protocol with the existing of MAC protocol
GTSNetS	Scalable, highly extensible and customizable; Enables the simulation of sensor control networks; Supports a large variety of TCP-based applications; Provides a robust interface for creating network graphs	Requires extensive centralized computational power; Requires huge memory as the Network scale increased

OPNET	Object-orientated, developed for military applications; Suitable for heterogeneous networks with various protocols; Uses a hierarchical strategy to organize the models	Quite expensive for commercial usage; Limited in scalability and extensibility
J-Sim	Designed around a component structure; Overcome the scalability issues inherent in object-orientated structures	Relatively complicated to use; No real established user base; Not widely adopted
SENSE	Built upon J-Sim simulator; Providing a component-orientated architecture; Improving on the inter-communication efficiency of J-Sim	Lacks of developed extensibility; Does not include functionality such as sensing
TOSSIM	It is both a simulator and an emulator for WSNs; Provides obvious advantages for projects deals with MICA nodes	All nodes in the network must run identical code; The network environment is not modeled

2.4.1 Classification

The classification that we propose provides a general overview of clustering design choices and attained performance. The classification criteria include the clustering purpose, assumptions, decision range, decision metrics, degree of mobility, number of clusters and complexity. We analyse each criterion in turn and describe the associated categories.

1. Purpose:

Clustering algorithms for ad-hoc and sensor networks improve network scalability by handling two important problems regarding the size and mobility of the network: they make a large network appear smaller, and a highly dynamic topology appear less dynamic [87]. Delay and message overhead represent the cost for clustering. In this section, we focus on the above described scalability improvements and show their direct benefits.

A large network appears smaller

Grouping nodes into clusters leads to having restricted communication and data exchange, which improves on the following network operations:

- *Medium access control (MAC)*. The access to the medium can be controlled and bandwidth can be allocated separately in each cluster, thus reducing the scope of inter-cluster interactions and avoiding redundant exchange of messages [82].
- *Routing*. The size of the routing tables is reduced by maintaining routes only to the cluster-heads, and not to every node in the network [131].
- *Flooding*. The cost of flooding is reduced by decreasing the number of nodes that broadcast the message to only cluster-heads and border nodes [121].
- *Data collection*. The data collected within a cluster is aggregated at the cluster-head and transmitted as a whole to the base station, thus avoiding excessive message exchange [52].
- *Service discovery*. The cluster-heads maintain a service directory for nodes in their cluster. Thus, service discovery messages are transmitted only to the cluster-head nodes, and not in the whole network [85].

A highly dynamic topology appears less dynamic

Clustering can be used to partition the network with the objective of maintaining a relatively stable topology. This improves on the following network functionalities:

- *Routing*. Complete routing information is maintained only for intra-cluster routing. Inter cluster routing is achieved by hiding the topology details within a cluster from external nodes, thus limiting far-reaching reactions to topology dynamics [87].
- *Collaborative processing*. Identifying nodes moving together and creating clusters based on joint movement allows for long-term intra-cluster collaborative processing.

Abstracting from the above specific purposes, several clustering algorithms are *generic* algorithms, meaning that they do not follow any particular objective, but rather propose a general solution that can be applied to various networking operations [121].

2. Assumptions

The general assumptions of clustering algorithms are that the wireless communication is reliable (that can be achieved by using a reliable transport protocol [138]), and that the communication links are symmetrical. In addition, each clustering algorithm has a list of specific assumptions, based on the functionality that the lower layers of the communication stack (MAC, routing, transport) or other algorithms running on the nodes provide. Additional assumptions include the following:

- *Synchronization*. Clustering algorithms that require a series of coordinated phases among the network nodes assume the availability of a network synchronization mechanism [52].
- *Unique node IDs*. Weight-based clustering algorithms require unique IDs assigned to nodes, which can be used to break ties [14].
- *Localization*. Localization information represents the coordinates of the node location. This information is useful for grouping nodes based on their location [121].
- *Level of dynamics*. The level of dynamics, such as a generic stationary/mobile attribute or the concrete node speed is useful for reasoned cluster membership selection [27].
- *Global information*. The number of nodes within the network or the total remaining energy represent global information, which can be useful for achieving the desired clustering structure [52].
- *Routing information*. Routing tables may be needed to ease the communication among nodes during cluster organization [87].
- *Additional hardware capabilities*. Hardware capabilities can help achieve a better clustering structure by providing additional information about neighbouring nodes or improved communication abilities. Examples include the capability to measure the Received Signal Strength (RSSI) and the availability of multiple transmission power levels [52, 151].
- *Additional structures*. Additional structures such as spanning trees may facilitate the clustering process, but may also induce more overhead for maintenance [137].
- *Additional algorithms*. Additional algorithms include localized event detection, context-sharing, availability paths or distance between pairs of nodes. The output of these algorithms is semantic information used for clustering decisions [27].

Some of the above mentioned assumptions are in line with the decision metrics used to form clusters, such as unique node IDs or additional algorithms. Other assumptions are used to improve the clustering result by exploiting the availability of specialized hardware, or taking advantage of additional information, such as location or routing tables.

3. Decision Metrics

The decision to become cluster-head or to join an existing cluster is typically based on the following metrics:

- *Time.* A node may become cluster-head on a time-dependent basis, i.e. if it is the first one in its neighbourhood that declares itself as cluster-head [43].
- *Probability.* A node may become cluster-head depending on a probabilistic measure. The probability is defined such that the desired number of cluster-heads is reached without the need of global message exchange. The probability may depend on the number of nodes in the network, global aggregate energy, local residual energy, number of times the nodes has been cluster-head, cluster size, etc [52].
- *Weight.* A weight is an application-specific number assigned to every node in the network. The weight may depend on multiple measures, such as the node degree, distance to neighbours, movement speed, energy left, capability. The node ID is usually used to break ties. A node may become a cluster-head if it has the highest weight among a group of nodes, depending on the decision range. Similarly, a node may choose to join the cluster-head with the highest weight [85]. Contrary to the probability metrics, weight metrics are deterministic.
- *Semantics.* Semantic properties refer to the relationship between pairs of nodes or among nodes in a group. Semantic properties include distance between nodes, availability paths between nodes, similar or relative mobility, location attribute or type of event detected. Clusters can be formed based on similar semantic properties of nodes [87].

The decision process may depend on more than one of the above metrics. For example, the cluster-head may be probabilistically selected, but the ordinary nodes choose a cluster-head based on a semantic property (e.g. the minimum distance to the neighbouring cluster-heads) [52]. Similarly, nodes are grouped based on semantic information, but the cluster-head is chosen depending on the weight.

4. Decision Range

The decision that each node takes is either autonomous, such that it does not depend on any other node in the network, or non-autonomous, where there are also other nodes that determine or influence the cluster membership. This set of nodes is denoted with the decision range. The decision range can vary from as little as only 1-hop neighbours [85], to as large as the whole network [27].

5. Mobility

The design of a clustering algorithm depends on the degree of dynamics expected to be present in the wireless network. The network can be:

- *Mobile*. The clustering algorithm is designed to handle network mobility during any of its phases [85, 14].
- *Quasi-static*. The network is assumed to be static during the initial cluster setup phase. Strategies for cluster maintenance are given for the subsequent phases [14].
- *Static*. The network is static. Changes of topology rarely occur and do not represent the focus of the clustering algorithm [52].

A clustering algorithm designed for quasi-static or static networks has as main purpose to increase the scalability of the network with respect to the number of nodes. Algorithms that take mobility into account focus on reducing both the size and dynamics of the network.

6. Disjoint Clusters

Depending whether a node may be part of one or more clusters, the output of the clustering algorithm falls in one of the following categories:

- *Disjoint clusters*. A node may belong to only one cluster [14].
- *Overlapping clusters*. A node may belong to more than one cluster [147].

Algorithms that partition the network into clusters and construct connected dominating sets of cluster-heads have as result overlapping clusters. The reason is that the nodes that connect a set of clusters (gateway nodes) belong to all the adjacent connected clusters. Disjoint clusters are generally constructed when a node has to share a piece of information (such as id, sensed data, service offer) with the cluster-head. The cluster-head is thus responsible to make use of this information on behalf of the node.

7. Number and Size of Clusters

Since clustering improves the scalability of higher layer protocols by making a large network appear smaller (see Section 2.4.1), the number and size of clusters is an important metric in characterizing the performance of a given algorithm. However, when speaking about performance, it is important to relate to the application objectives. In some cases, it is desirable to have a small number of clusters (for example to route packets quickly between clusters), but in other cases it is important to keep the cluster size small and consequently they form more clusters (for example to manage the structure in the presence of mobility).

Algorithms generate different cluster sizes, depending for example on the number of nodes in the network *n*, the average node degree *D* [14] or the probability *p* of becoming a cluster-head [52]. The number and size of clusters generated by semantic algorithms depend on the number of distinct semantic properties that represent clustering criteria. Algorithms that con-struct weakly connected dominating sets usually use the approximation factor (the ratio between approximate and optimal solution) as a metric to characterize the performance of the algorithm [147].

8. Complexity

The complexity of a clustering algorithm is essential for estimating the latency and message overhead involved in building and maintaining the clusters.

To evaluate the *time complexity*, the algorithm is considered to start from a stable state. An event of a single, isolated change in this network (e.g. a link added or deleted) triggers a series of steps for restructuring the structure [17]. The time it takes for the algorithm, after this event to achieve a valid cluster structure is denoted as convergence time.

The *message complexity* defines the communication effort for creating and maintaining clusters [17]. For achieving minimum energy expenditure and processing load on the nodes, the overhead induced by clustering messages should be as low as possible.

2.4.2 A Comparison among Various Clustering Algorithms

This section shows a comparison of different clustering algorithms in terms of the purpose, decision neighbourhood rang, mobility, and finally whether the clusters are disjoint or not. By analysing Table 2.2, we can observe that most of the existing clustering algorithms are less suitable for mobile environment [86]. The reasons for that are: Firstly, electing the cluster-heads based on information from nodes which are multiple hopes away leads to high overhead and slow reaction to topology changes. Secondly, maintaining complete intra-cluster information is an expensive task which results in a high traffic. Thirdly, the complexity of the multi-layer clustering algorithms leads to a lot of efforts in building and maintaining the desired structure.

2.5 Summary

Clustering algorithms for ad-hoc and sensor networks improve network scalability by handling two important problems regarding the size and mobility of the network. They make a large network appear smaller, and a highly dynamic topology appears less dynamic.

The design of a clustering algorithm depends on the degree of dynamics expected to be present in the wireless network. The network can be: Mobile, Quasi-static or Static.

The output of the clustering algorithm falls in one of the following categories: Disjoint clusters. A node may belong to only one cluster. Overlapping clusters. A node may belong to more than one cluster.

The high overhead and slow reaction to topology changes of WSNs led to make the task of designing a clustering algorithm for mobile WSN is a challenging task. In this chapter, a general overview for Wireless Sensor Networks; types, classification and features are presented.

Table 2.2: A Comparison of Clustering Algorithms

Algorithm	Purpose	Decision neigh-bour-hood range	Mobility	Disjoint Clusters
WCA [27]	MAC	Network wide	Mobile	Yes
LEACH [52]	Data collection	1-hop	Static	Yes
HEED [151]	Routing	1-hop	Quasi static	Yes
MOCA [152]	Data collection	k-hops	Static	No
Coyle et al. [12]	Data collection	k-hops	Static	Yes
EEMC [65]	Data collection	1-hop	Static	Yes
Bouhafs et al. [21]	Data collection	Network wide	Static	No
Tandem [84]	Collaborative processing	1-hop	Mobile	Yes
Smart clustering [122]	Routing	1-hop	Quasi static	Yes
Wang et al. [139]	Information dec-imation	Network wide	Quasi static	Yes

Comparison with other types of wireless networks is also discussed. The major hardware constraints of sensors' platforms and the challenges for this type of networks are explained.

Description for the most popular simulators used to analyse and evaluate the networks algorithms are explored.

The clustered topology for the WSNs with general assumptions for clustering algorithms and a comparison among various clustering algorithms is also demonstrated.

Chapter 3

Swarm Intelligence

3.1 Introduction

Swarm Intelligence (SI) indicates a recent computational and behavioural metaphor for solving distributed problems that originally took its inspiration from the biological examples provided by social insects (ants, termites, bees, wasps) and by swarming, flocking, herding behaviours in vertebrates [70]. It is an attempt to design algorithms or distributed problem-solving devices inspired by the collective behaviour of social insects and other animal societies. The common behaviours in all kinds of swarms are [70, 19, 39];

- Control is fully distributed among a number of individuals;
- Communications among the individuals happen in a localized way;
- System-level behaviours appear to transcend the behavioural repertoire of the single individual; and
- The overall response of the system is quite robust and adaptive with respect to changes in the environment.

Swarm intelligence (SI) as defined by Bonabeau, Dorigo and Theraulaz is "any attempt to design algorithms or distributed problem-solving devices inspired by the collective behaviour of social insect colonies and other animal societies" [19]. The term "swarm" is used in a general sense to refer to any such loosely structured collection of interacting agents. The classic example of a swarm is a swarm of bees, but the metaphor of a swarm can be extended to other systems with a similar architecture. An ant colony can be thought of as a swarm whose individual agents are ants, a flock of birds is a swarm whose agents are birds, traffic is a swarm of cars, a crowd is a swarm of people, an immune system is a swarm of cells and molecules, and an economy is a swarm of economic agents. Although the notion of a swarm suggests an aspect of collective motion in space, as in the swarm of a flock of birds, all types of collective behaviour are considered here, not just spatial motion.

3.2 Swarm Intelligence in Nature

Swarm behaviour in nature is divided into two categories: *Species* whose individuals form a swarm because they benefit in some way and *Social insects* which live in colonies whose members cannot survive on their own [39].

3.2.1 Social Insects

If we compare the complexity of the buildings and actions of the colony to the relative simplicity of an individual it will be a striking feature of social insects. Termite builders are one kind of self-organizing system. There is no central control, the intention of the population is distributed throughout its membership and the members themselves are unaware of the "plan" they are carrying out. Actors in the system follow simple rules, and improbable structures emerge from lower-level activities, analogous to the way gliders emerge from simple rules in a cellular automaton.

It appears that the termites build a dome by taking some dirt in their mouths, moistening it, and following these rules:

- Move in the direction of the strongest pheromone concentration.
- Deposit what you are carrying where the smell is strongest.

After some random movements searching for a relatively strong pheromone field, the termites will have started a number of small pillars as shown in Figure 3.1 [39]. The pillars signify places where a greater number of termites have recently passed, and thus the pheromone concentration is high there. The pheromone dissipates with time, so in order for it to accumulate, the number of termites must exceed some threshold; they must leave pheromones faster than the chemicals evaporate. This prevents the formation of a great number of pillars, or of a wasteland strewn with little mouthfuls of dirt.

Figure 3.1: Termites' nest (© Masson) [39]

Ants manage to efficiently search an area for food whether it is evenly distributed or scattered in patches. Figure 3.2 from [19] shows an example for the robustness of the insect colony. There is some degree of communication among the ants, just enough to keep them from wandering off completely at random. By this minimal communication they can remind each other that they are not alone but are cooperating with team-mates. It takes a large number of ants, all reinforcing each other this way, to sustain any activity-such as trail building-for any length of time.

Social insects also effectively divide tasks among individuals like finding food, feeding the brood and defending the nest. All this is not achieved by central control but by *stigmergy* and very seldom by one to one communication. Stigmergy is communication by altering the state of the environment in a way that will affect the behaviours of others for whom the environment is a stimulus. It describes an indirect communication by leaving marks in the environment. These marks can be the structures that are built or markers meant especially for the purpose of communication (typically pheromones which can be smelled by the individuals). The marks left by the colony act as stimuli for the individuals and can trigger certain actions. Additionally, the termites are guided by pheromone concentration forming for example the pattern for the royal chamber around the queen.

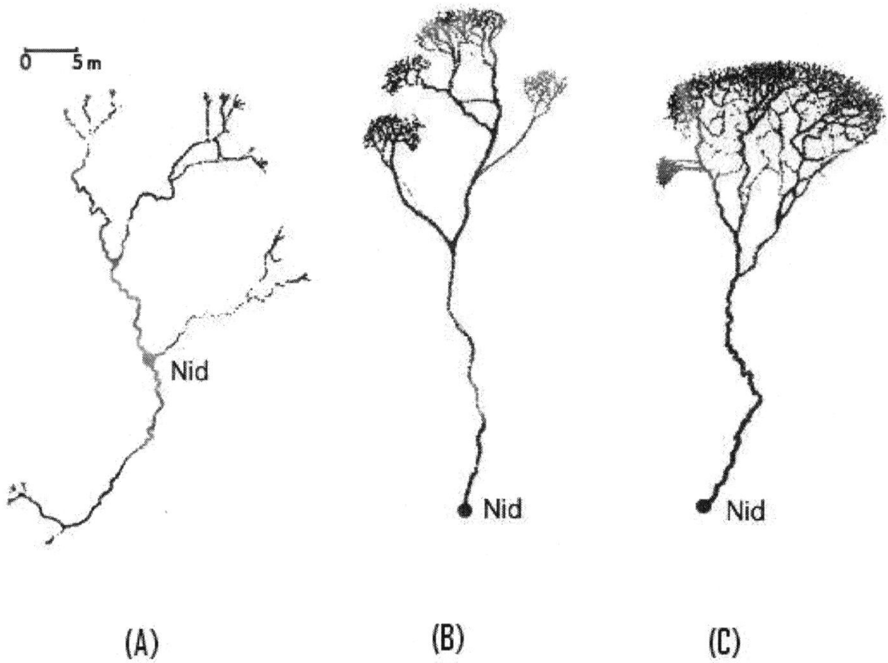

Figure 3.2: Foraging patterns of three army ant species: The food of (A) is distributed in patches while for (B) has an intermediary distribution. (C) is evenly distributed. [19]

3.2.2 Flocks, Herds and Schools

Social insects can not survive without living as swarms. The advantages for herd animals, flocks of birds and schools of fish to form swarms is to defence against predators (see Figure 3.3) [110]. As Kenward [73] showed the success of hawk attacks on pigeons decreases greatly with the size of the swarm.

Although the disadvantage of sharing food sources can be outweighed by the reduced chances of finding no food at all, whenever the food is unpredictably distributed in patches, individuals may also increase their chances of finding a mate [46] and for animals that travel great distances, like migratory birds and certain fish species, there is a decrease in energy consumption when moving in a tight formation.

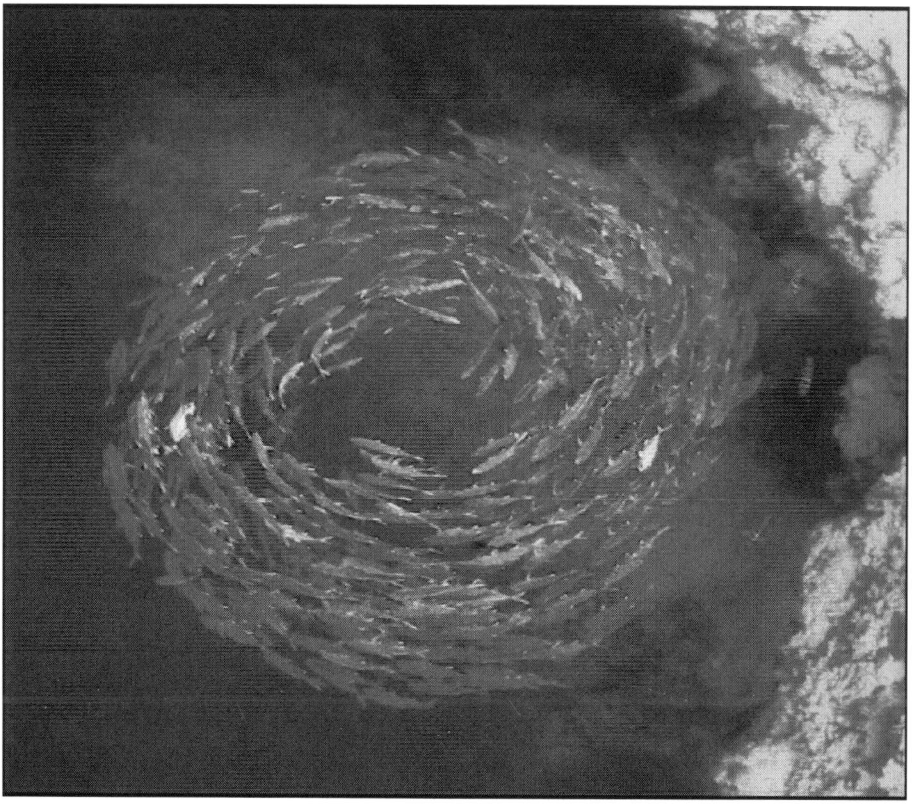

Figure 3.3: Fish schooling (© CORO, CalTech) [113]

As flocks, herds and schools can become very large and the individuals are both limited in their mental capacity and their perception, it can be assumed that only simple, local rules control the movements of a single animal. "Local" means that only objects in a certain neighbourhood, depending on the perception of the individual, are taken into account. The most basic behaviours seem to be an urge to stay close to the swarm and one to avoid collisions [70]. The perception is of course not the same for different species resulting in a different range of possible swarm behaviours. Fish for example cannot see as far as birds especially in murky water but can feel the pressure waves of neighbours with their lateral line organ [104]. Birds on the other hand have long-range vision enabling them to see the movements of far away flock mates. This enables them to prepare for the change of direction, which explains the quick propagation of "manoeuvre waves" going through a flock that is much faster than can be explained by strictly local rules and the reaction times of the birds [107] (see Figure 3.4).

Figure 3.4: Birds flocking in V-formation (© CORO, CalTech) [110]

Computer simulations have been created after these findings. Reynolds [110] created a computer graphics simulation of swarms which he called the *boids2* model using three simple local rules for the movement of an individual: Collision Avoidance, Velocity Matching (heading and speed) and Flock Centring (see Figure 3.5). Heppner and Grenander [55] independently developed a similar model using stochastic nonlinear differential equations [10]. Swarms in nature could be said to "run in constant time" because every individual interacts only with its neighbours and therefore its mental capacity does not limit the size of the swarm. In the simulation the relations to all other individuals have to be taken into account, at least to determine if they are in the neighbourhood.

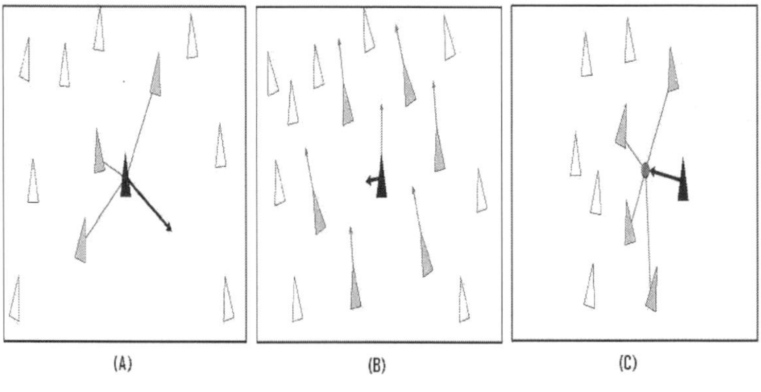

Figure 3.5: Rules for the boids simulation: (A) Collision Avoidance. (B) Velocity Matching. (C) Flock Centring.

3.3 Metaheuristics

The term *meta-heuristics*, first used by Glover [45], contains all heuristics methods that show evidence of achieving good quality solutions for a problem of interest within an acceptable time. Usually, metaheuristics offer no guarantee of obtaining the global best solutions [46].

The interaction between computer science and optimization has yielded new practical solvers for global optimization problems, called *meta-heuristics*. The structures of meta-heuristics are mainly based on simulating nature and artificial intelligence tools. Metaheuristics mainly invoke exploration and exploitation search procedures in order to diversify the search all over the search space and intensify the search in some promising areas. Therefore, metaheuristics cannot easily be entrapped in local minima. However, metaheuristics are computationally costly due to their slow convergence. One of the main reasons for their slow convergence is that they may fail to detect promising search directions especially in the vicinity of local minima due to their random constructions.

In terms of the process of updating solutions, meta-heuristics can be classified into two classes; population-based methods and point-to-point methods. In the latter methods, the search keeps only one solution at the end of each iteration, from which the search will start in the next iteration. On the other hand, the population-based methods keep a set of many solutions at the end of each iteration.

In terms of search methodologies and trial solutions generation, meta-heuristics can be categorized into several groups of methods, as shown in Figure 3.6 [50]. Among those methods, we are mainly exploring some of the Evolutionary Algorithms (EAs) and Swarm Intelligence (SI) metaheuristics in the following sections because our ENAMS Algorithm is based on it.

3.4 Evolutionary Algorithms (EAs)

Evolutionary Algorithms (EAs) tries to mimic the evolution of a species. Specifically, EAs simulate the biological processes that allow the consecutive generations in a population to adapt to their environment [50]. The adaptation process is mainly applied through genetic inheritance from parents to children and through survival of the fittest.

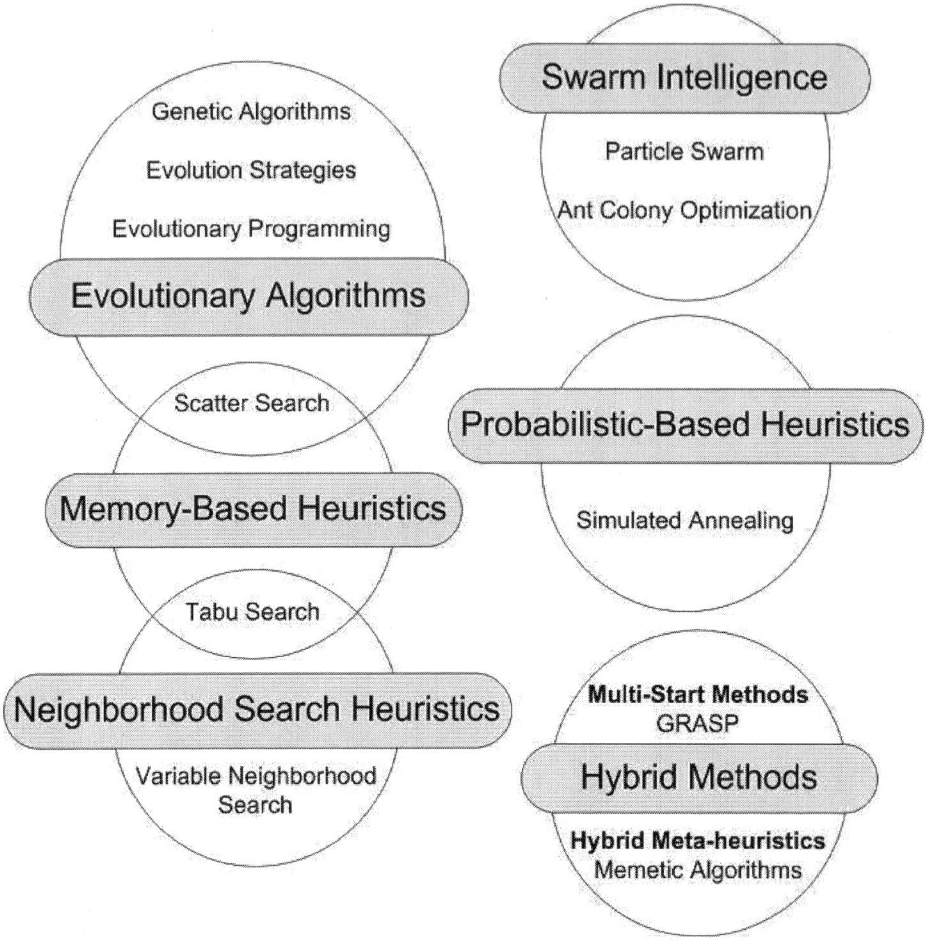

Figure 3.6: Classification of Meta-heuristics [51]

The main types of EAs are; Genetic Algorithms, Evolution Strategies, Evolutionary Programming, and Scatter Search. In contrast to other EAs, Scatter Search invokes more artificial elements, like using memory elements to update populations.

3.4.1 Genetic Algorithms (GAs)

In the past few decades, Genetic Algorithms (GAs) have been used in science to derive solutions for a wide range of optimization problems such as; construction of wind turbines [15], pattern-recognition systems [7], multi-processor task scheduling [75], energy optimization [59, 141], self organization of sensors networks [74], and travelling salesman problems [117].

Genetic Algorithms are efficient search algorithms that simulate the adaptive evolution process of natural systems [113]. They represents a stochastic search procedures based on the mechanics of natural selection, genetics, and evolution [47]. Since they simultaneously evaluate many points in the search space, they are more likely to find the global solution of a given problem. In addition, they use only a simple scalar performance measure that does not require or use derivative information, so they are general-purpose optimization methods for solving search problems. Two major primary areas in which GAs have been employed; optimization and machine learning. In machine learning, GAs have been successfully applied to the learning of neural networks [60, 146] and fuzzy systems [34, 35].

In GAs, a candidate solution for a specific problem is called an individual or a chromosome and consists of a linear list of genes, each individual represents a point in the search space, hence it will be a possible solution to the problem [66]. A population consists of a finite number of individuals. Each individual is decided by an evaluating mechanism to obtain its fitness value. Based on this fitness value and undergoing genetic operators, a new population is generated iteratively with each successive population referred to as a generation.

The GAs use three basic operators (reproduction, crossover, and mutation) to manipulate the genetic composition of a population. Reproduction is a process by which the most highly rated individuals in the current generation are reproduced in the new generation.

The crossover operator produces two offsprings (new candidate solutions) by recombining the information from two parents. There are two processing steps in this operation. In the first step, a given number of crossing sites are selected uniformly, along with the parent individual at random. In the second step, two new individuals are formed by exchanging alternate pairs of selection between the selected sites.

Mutation is a random alteration of some gene values in an individual. The allele of each gene is a candidate for mutation, and its function is determined by the mutation probability. Many efforts on the enhancement of traditional GAs have been proposed [90]. Among them, one category focuses on modifying the structure of the population or the role an individual plays in it [8, 125], such as distributed GA [123], cellular GA [32], and symbiotic GA [91]. Another category aims to modify the basic operations, such as crossover or mutation, of traditional GAs [145, 132].

Algorithm 1 illustrates the basic process in GAs.

Initialization: Generate random population of n chromosomes
while *the stop condition is not satisfied* **do**
  Evaluate the fitness $g(x)$ of each chromosome x in the population;
  while *the new population is not complete* **do**
    Selection: Select two parent chromosomes from a population according to their fi
    Crossover: With a crossover probability, crossover the parents to form a new offspring (children);
    Mutation: With a mutation probability mutate new offspring;
    Accepting: Place new offspring in a new population;
  end
  Replace: Use new generated population for further runs;
end
Return: the best solution of the current population;

Algorithm 1: Basic Process in Genetic Algorithms

3.5 Swarm Intelligence (SI) - Metaheuristics

The SI-metaheuristic is an arbitrary problem solving strategy which falls under the SI-definition. It is inspired by the "behaviour of social insect colonies and other animal societies" [70]. The main two SI-metaheuristics are; Ant Colony Optimization (ACO) and Particle Swarm Optimization (PSO). The ACO is briefly introduced in the following Section. The PSO will be explored in more details in Section(3.5.2) since it constitutes an important part of our ENAMS algorithm.

3.5.1 Ant Colony Optimization

Ant colony optimization is a metaheuristic for difficult combinatorial optimization problems modelled after the stigmergetic communication of ants finding shortest paths to food sources [38]. The first ACO-algorithm was Ant System (AS), introduced by Dorigo [37] in 1992. He later generalized it into the ACO meta-heuristic. Ant colony optimization uses virtual ants laying out virtual pheromone in the problem states they visit. As in nature the virtual ants communicate indirectly and the solution to the problem emerges by the cooperation of the colony. As an example a simple implementation for the travelling salesman problem (TSP) could work as follows: Ants start at a random city and choose the next city stochastically but prefer the road with more pheromone. When they cannot choose another city or have completed a tour, they die. If they managed to complete a tour they deposit pheromone on all the visited edges. The shorter the tour, the more pheromone is placed.

Ants use pheromones to find shortest paths to food sources. They lay out pheromone trails behind them and prefer regions with higher pheromone concentration when deciding where to go. Some species deposit different amounts of pheromone depending whether they are on the way to or back from the food source and depending on its size.

As ants taking the shorter path will reinforce the trail more often the pheromone concentration rises and the path will be preferred by following individuals (see Figure 3.7) [54]. This self-energizing effect leads to the development of a short-est path used by the individuals. Pheromone evaporation prevents stagnation, allowing for dynamic changes in the environment. It also avoids premature convergence on a not optimal path.

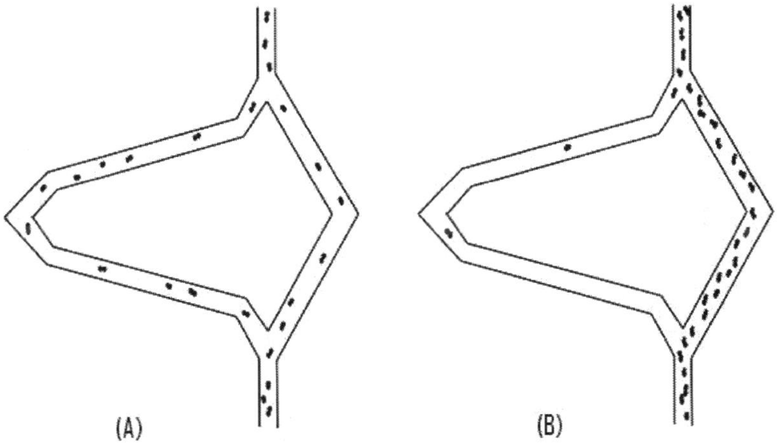

Figure 3.7: Ants find the shorter path in an experimental setup. A bridge leads from a nest to a foraging area. (A) 4 minutes after bridge placement. (B) 8 minutes after bridge placement.

Ants work simultaneously and new ants are created as needed to keep the population on a desired level. The search is finished when a short enough tour is found, or a maximum number of iterations were done.

3.5.2 Particle Swarm Optimization (PSO)

Particle Swarm Optimization (PSO) is a population based stochastic optimization technique developed by Kennedy and Eberhart in 1995 [71], inspired by social behaviour of bird flocking or fish schooling. PSO shares many similarities with evolutionary computation techniques such as Genetic Algorithms (GAs). The system is initialized with a population of random solutions and searches for optima by updating generations. However, unlike GAs, PSO has no evolution operators such as crossover and mutation.

Definitions:

In PSO, a problem is modelled as an n-dimensional solution space and a population of particles search through this n-dimensional space for optimal solutions.

Definition 1. In PSO, a particle P_i simulates an individual in a bird flock. Figure 3.8 shows a group of particles in a 2-dimensional space. Each particle in the group is responsible for searching and keeping solutions together with its fellow particles. At any time t, particle P_i is located at some position $x_i(t)$ in the n-dimensional problem space. Conventionally, $x_i(t)$ indicates the current position of P_i and $x_i(t-1)$ represents the previous position.

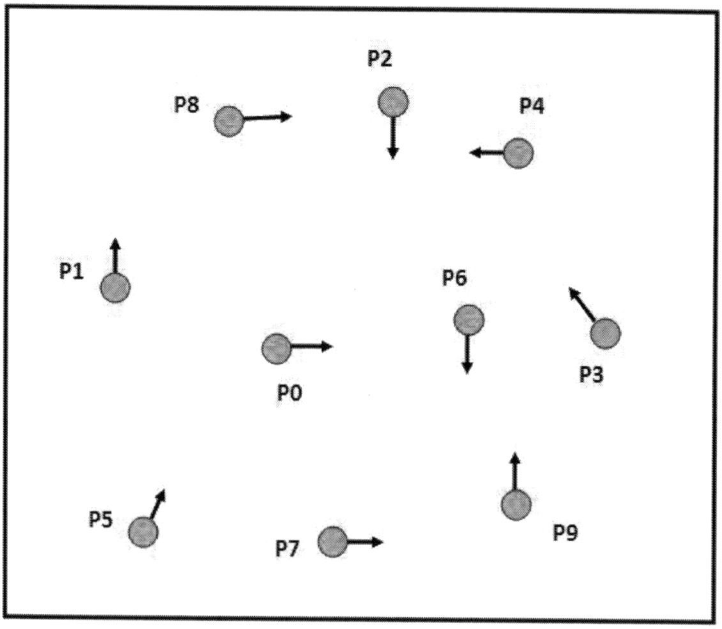

Figure 3.8: Particle swarm (population = 10) in a 2-dimensional space

In the problem solving context, a particle with its position represents a potential solution.

Definition 2. In PSO, a swarm $P = P_1, P_2, ...P_s$ is a set of particles.

Definition 3. A particle's velocity $\overrightarrow{v}(t) = [u_1, u_2..., u_n]$ is an n-dimensional vector that moves particle *Pi* at time t as shown in Figure 3.9. Mathematically, the position-velocity relation is:

$$x_i(t) = x_i(t-1) + \vec{v}(t) \tag{3.1}$$

In PSO, velocities are mainly affected by particle's own knowledge and the neighbours' experience.

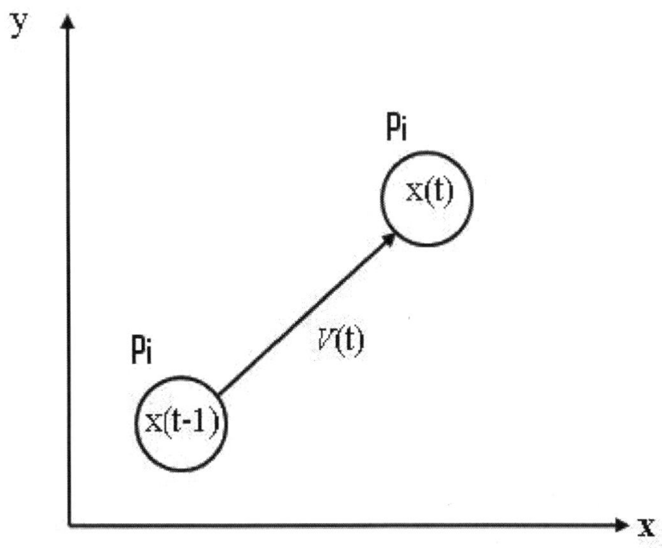

Figure 3.9: The position-velocity relation in a 2-dimensional space

Conceptually, a velocity $\vec{v}(t)$ can be derived from the relation in Equation 3.2, where $\phi 1$ and $\phi 2$ are parameters as will be discussed in Section (3.5.3). According to this relation, a velocity can be computed using:

$$\vec{v}(t) = \phi_1(individual\_experience) + \phi_2(global\_experience) \tag{3.2}$$

Definition 4. A *neighbourhood* defines the social structure of a swarm and indicates which ones a particle should interact with. Within a neighbourhood, particles interact, communicate and share information. To form a neighbourhood, we may not restrict to the physical distances between particles; in fact, they are often defined by the enumeration labels of the particles in PSO. For example in Figure 3.10 from [41], nine particles are enumerated as $P_1, P_2, \ldots P_9$. Regardless of the physical distance, P_1, P_2 and P_3 are a neighbour of size three, P_4, P_5 and P_6 form another neighbour of size three, and this is the same for P_7, P_8 and P_9. Stars, rings and wheels are the most commonly used neighbourhood structures (shown in Figure 3.11.)

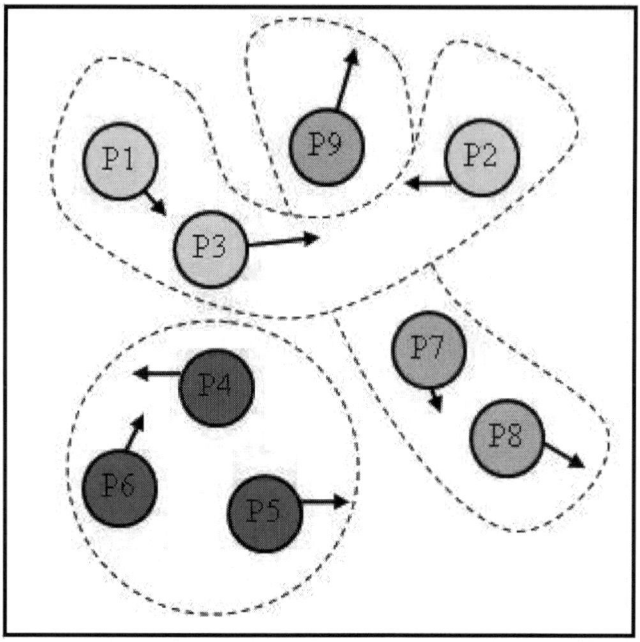

Figure 3.10: A global swarm vs. local neighbourhoods [41]

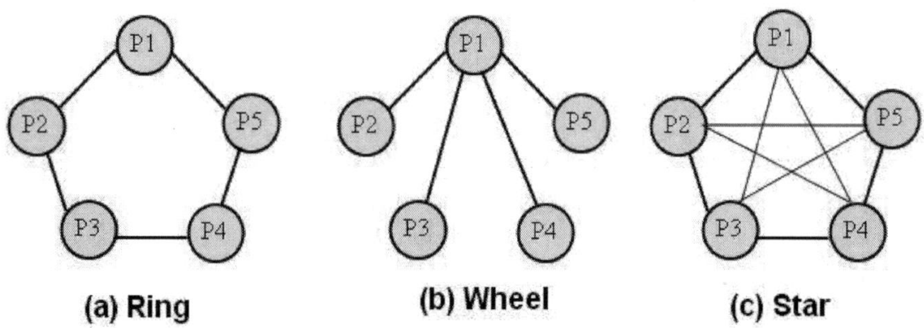

Figure 3.11: Simple neighbourhood topologies (population = 5)

In the PSO context, two terms, local versus global are often used. "Local" refers to an individual neighbourhood while the "global" refers to the entire swarm as one big neighbourhood. For example, there are three local neighbourhoods in Figure 3.10. Neighbourhoods can overlap and a particle can belong to multiple neighbourhoods. For instance, particles P_1, P_2, P_3, P_4 and P_5 are to form neighbourhoods of size (3) in a Ring topology as shown in Figure 3.11 (a). We may have five neighbourhoods in total: {P_1, P_2, P_3}, {P_2, P_3, P_4}, {P_3, P_4, P_5}, {P_4, P_5, P_1} and {P_5, P_1, P_2}. A particle in such a structure retrieves information from another two particles directly connected to it.

Different neighbourhood structures may affect the performance of the swarm. They determine how information propagate among particles, and thus may affect the convergence of particles, i.e. when and how particles may come together, arrive at some stable state and stop improving the solution. That is, particles may converge on different local optima or at different time with different neighbourhood topologies. In a star topology as shown in Figure 3.11 (c), all particles are influenced by one global best location so far in every iteration and move towards the location, so they tend to converge quickly to the global best. In a ring topology, the neighbourhood segments are overlapped so the convergence may spread from one neighbourhood to another and eventually pull all the particles together.

By gradually spreading information, the swarm converges slower in a ring than in a star. For a swarm in a wheel, there exists one and only one central particle, which serves as a buff [70]. The central particle collects and compares the positions of all particles, finds the best one and moves itself towards the best position. All other particles then pull information from the central particle and start moving towards the same position. Because of this buff effect, a wheel topology may preserve diversity for a bit longer and prevent the swarm from converging too fast on local optima.

3.5.3 Continuous PSO

PSO was originally designed to optimize continuous nonlinear mathematical functions, and so it deals with real numbers [71]. The algorithm randomly initializes each particle P_i to position $x_i(0)$ and velocity $\vec{v}(0)$. At each time step t, every particle calculates a new velocity $\vec{v}(t)$ based on the social-psychological tendency [41, 71] from both its own and its neighbours' knowledge. Considering different ways of sharing information, there can be three ways to compute velocities:

1. Individual *pbest* only or one particle per neighbourhood: each particle makes decisions on its own, and ignores everybody else.

   $$\vec{v}(t) = w\,\vec{v}(t-1) + r_1c_1(xpbest - x_i(t-1)) \quad (3.3)$$

2. Global *gbest* and individual pbest: every particle considers the knowledge of all particles within a single neighbourhood.

   $$\vec{v}(t) = w\,\vec{v}(t-1)+r_1c_1(xpbest-x_i(t-1))+r_2c_2(xgbest-x_i(t-1)) \quad (3.4)$$

3. Local neighbourhoods *lbest* and particle individual pbest: suppose particle Pi is in neighbourhood k.

   $$\vec{v}(t) = w\,\vec{v}(t-1)+r_1c_1(xpbest-x_i(t-1))+r_2c_2(xlbest_k-x_i(t-1)) \quad (3.5)$$

where w is a parameter to control how much the new velocity is affected by the previous velocity. r_1 and r_2 are random numbers in [0, 1] to randomize the influence of group experience and particles' individual experience. c_1 and c_2 are positive acceleration constants.

Once the new velocity has been determined, particle P_i updates its position using Equation(3.1) mentioned earlier. Then iteratively, all particles keep updating the velocities and their positions until timeout or the goal fitness value is obtained.

In short, this algorithm makes use of a swarm of particles stochastically and intelligently exploring new regions and exploiting towards the previous better regions until the swarm reaches an "optimum". The particles intelligence comes from social interaction and information sharing, and such learning abilities dominate the PSO algorithm [70].

3.5.4 Discrete PSO

Kennedy and Eberhart's discrete model [72] is a version of the PSO that does not directly use real numbers. It makes the PSO applicable to problems with variable values taken from a discrete domain e.g. $v \in 1, 1.5, 2, 2.5, 3$ as opposed to over a continuous range $1 \leq v \leq 3$ where there are infinite number of values between any two numbers. The rationale is that not all problems can be described using continuous domains; for example, the graph colouring has finite domains such as (red, blue, green).

In Kennedy and Eberhart's discrete PSO, a particle and its position still represent a solution in the problem solution space. Instead of consisting of a sequence of integers or real numbers however, a particle *Pi*'s position $x_i(t)$ at time t is composed of a bit-string: $x_{i1}(t), x_{i2}(t) \ldots, x_{in}(t)$ where $x_{ij}(t) \in \{0, 1\}$ for each $j \in \{1, 2, \ldots n\}$. Also, in order to derive the bit value of $x_{ij}(t)$, a velocity element $v_{ij}(t)$ is not directly used as an increment to compute $x_{ij}(t)$, rather it is used as a threshold to determine the possibility of a bit change. More specifically, $v_{ij}(t)$ is transformed by a sigmoid function and then compared with a uniformly distributed random number $\rho_{ij}(t) \in [0, 1]$.

$$x(t+1) = \begin{cases} 0 \text{ if } \rho_{ij}(t) \geq \dfrac{1}{1+\exp(-v_{ij}(t))}, \\ 1 \qquad \textit{otherwise.} \end{cases} \tag{3.6}$$

3.5.5 Modified PSO Models

In recent times, there have been a number of improvements to the original PSO. We have explored different versions of PSO where the extension to the original algorithm is distinct from each other. The following sections describes the PSO versions which are studied in this research.

1. PSO - Time Varying Inertia Weight (TVIW)

PSO-TVIW is the same basic PSO algorithm, but with inertia weight varying with time from 0.9 to 0.4 and the acceleration coefficient is set to 2. The time varying inertia weight is mathematically represented as follows [114]:

$$w = (\text{weight} - 0.4) \times \frac{(MAXITER - iter)}{MAXITER} + 0.4 \tag{3.7}$$

where MAXITER is the maximum iteration allowed, *iter* is the current iteration number and weight is a constant set to 0.9.

2. PSO - Time Varying Acceleration Coefficients (TVAC)

PSO - TVAC proposed by Ratnaweera et al. [109], uses time varying acceleration coefficient (TVAC). The C_1 varies from 2.5 to 0.5 and the C_2 varies from 0.5 to 2.5. Here the cognitive component is reduced and social component is increased by changing C_1 and C_2. The large cognitive com-po-nent and the small social component in the initial stages of the algorithm helps the particle to wander around the search space. However, the small cognitive component and large social component at the later stages of the algorithm helps the particle to converge to the global optima. TVAC is mathematically represented as follows:

$$C_1 = (C_1min - C_1max)\frac{iter}{MAXITER} + C_1min \tag{3.8}$$

$$C_2 = (C_2min - C_2max)\frac{iter}{MAXITER} + C_2min \tag{3.9}$$

In Equations 3.8 and 3.9 C_1min and C_2min are constants set to 0.5, C_1max and C_2max are also constants set to 2.5. Thus, in this algorithm as the *iter* progresses, C_1 varies from 2.5 to 0.5 and C_2 varies from 0.5 to 2.5.

3. Hierarchical PSO with Time Varying Acceleration Coefficients (HPSO-TVAC)

In this method the particle's behaviour will not be influenced by the previous velocity term of Equation (4.5). Due to non-influence of previous velocity, re-initialisation of velocity is used when the velocity stagnates in the search space [109]. Therefore, in this method, a series of particle swarm optimisers are automatically generated inside the main particle swarm optimiser according to the behaviour of the particle in the search space, until the convergence criteria is met. The re-initialisation velocity is set proportional to $V\,max$. The pseudo code for re-initialising velocity is as follows:

$v_i^{k+1} = c_1 rand_1 * (pbest_i - s_i^k) + c_2 rand_2 * (gbest - s_i^k)$

$if\ (v_i^{k+1} == 0)$

$if\ (rand_1() < 0.5)$

$v_i^{k+1} = rand_2() * v$

$else$

$v_i^{k+1} = -rand_3() * v$

$endif$

$endif$

$v_i^{k+1} = sign(v_i^{k+1}) * min(fabs(v_i^{k+1}, v_{max}))$

where *randi*(), *i*= 1, 2, 3 are separately generated uniformly distributed random numbers in the range [0,1] and v is the re-initialisation velocity.

4. PSO with Supervisor-Student Model (PSO-SSM)

In this method Liu et al. [83] proposed PSO-SSM to achieve low computational costs. The algorithm introduces a new parameter called momentum factor (mc) to update the positions of particles. In this algorithm, they also proposed a different velocity updating mechanism from the conventional PSO algorithms. Here velocity is updated only if each particle's fitness at the current iteration is not better than that of previous iteration. The velocity serves as a navigator (supervisor) by getting the right direction, while the position (student) gets a right step size along the direction. The velocity and the position are modified using the following equations:

$$v_i^{k+1} = v_i^k + c_1 \mathrm{rand}_1 \times (pbest_i - s_i^k) + c_2 rand_2 \times (gbest - s_i^k) \quad (3.10)$$

$$x_i^{k+1} = (1 - mc) \times x_i^k + mc \times v_i^{k+1} \quad (3.11)$$

3.5.6 PSO Strengths

In the past few decades, PSO has been successfully applied in many research and application areas. It is demonstrated that PSO gets better results in a faster, cheaper way as compared with other optimization methods [22]. Another reason that PSO is attractive is that there are few parameters to adjust. One version, with slight variations, works well in a wide variety of applications. Particle swarm optimization has been used for approaches that can be used across a wide range of applications, as well as for specific applications focused on a specific requirement.

One reason for PSO gaining its popularity is that it is conceptually straightforward and computationally simple [70]. Simulating birds flocking, particle swarms fundamentally use two simple formulas to effectively search the goal. Also, research has shown that in comparing PSO with other algorithms on a variety of problems [31, 112, 18, 44, 153], it can perform better on some problems and be competitive on others. Since PSOs are a new search technique, much research has been targeting to improve the original PSOs for solving various problems and it has great potential to be done further. For example, owing to its similarity to evolutionary computation (EC) methods, many successful EC techniques and ideas may be integrated to improve PSOs.

Like many EC algorithms, PSO has a number of parameters to adjust. On one hand, this is beneficial for implementing adaptive systems [70] and also shows the extensibility of PSO to other specifically designed algorithms although it may not perform as well as those algorithms. On the other hand, tuning parameters for solving a particular problem or a range of problems can be time-consuming and non-trivial. Compared with EC methods, PSO does not have as many parameters to tune in order to get acceptable performance [58]. In addition, Hu and Eberthart suggest that PSO is applicable for both constrained and unconstrained problems even without pre-transforming the constraints and the objectives of a problem [58].

3.5.7 PSO Weaknesses

Researchers have found several issues that prevent the generic PSOs from effectively solving certain types of problems. Although the improvement has been working on to handle these issues, the solutions may not easily be applied to solve other problems; thus, we should keep these issues in mind while developing new particle swarms for solving other problems. For example, although PSO has the ability to converge quickly, it tends to wander and slow down as it approaches an optimum [135]. Owing to the premature convergence, it gets stuck quite easily and cannot explore wide enough. This can be problematic for solving multimodal problems where the problems have multiple optimal solutions.

Particularly if many of those optima are only local rather than global [135], particles may get trapped at local optima. In addition, while there are not many parameters to control [58] and as mentioned previously, these parameters open up a potential for developing adaptive PSO systems, some of the parameters are problem dependent. Some suggested values and experimental settings are still at trial-and-error stage [40], and it can be non-trivial to find the right settings for individual problems.

3.5.8 PSO Suitability for Energy Efficient Mobile WSNs

A particle swarm is a self-organizing system whose global dynamics emerge from local rules. As each individual trajectory is adjusted towards the successes of neighbours, the population converges or clusters in optimal regions of the search space. The search would fail if individuals did not influence one another; because a number of them are sharing information locally, it is possible to discover optima in the landscape [70].

Particle swarms have a unique way of using gradient information to guide their search. A particle moves in a stochastic oscillatory trajectory through the problem space, sampling around relatively optimal local points, while an evolutionary individual searches by changing position through mutation and crossover. This perpetuated directional movement through the search space gives particles their characteristic behaviour; their interaction results in effective search for optima [36].

One major difference between particle swarms and traditional evolutionary computation methods is that particles' velocities are adjusted, while evolutionary individuals' positions are acted upon; it is as if we were altering the "fate" rather than the "state" of particle swarm individuals [70].

3.6 Deployment of SI in WSNs

Continued advances of wireless communication technologies have enabled the deployment of large scale wireless sensor networks WSNs. Sensor nodes monitor the surroundings and process the data obtained and transmit this data to the base station located on the periphery of the sensor network. Each sensor node is equipped with a limited battery-supplied energy which makes energy consumption a critical issue.

Innovative techniques are highly required to improve energy efficiency and prolong the lifetime of WSNs. Many energy-efficient solutions have been proposed. An approach that is likely to succeed is the use of a hierarchical structure [12]. Clustering is an important technique in this respect which aims at generating the minimum number of clusters and transmission distance [53]. The clustering algorithms also distinguish themselves by how the cluster heads are elected. Clustering is an NP-hard problem [3]. For a given network it is always difficult to find an optimal cluster-head (CH) placement.

Clustering wireless sensor networks has been researched intensively in the last decade because this technique can greatly reduce communication cost of the network nodes since the sensors only need to send data to the nearest cluster-head. However, cluster-heads expends more energy than ordinary nodes because they are responsible of passing all the sensed information to the sink point (destination).

Heinzelman et al. in LEACH [53] proposed a clustering based on routing technique. Cluster head collects and aggregates data from member nodes and transmits the data to base station (sink). Member nodes only need sense the data and transmit to its cluster head. It is the basic concept of cluster-based routing protocol that sensor nodes play the role of cluster-head or cluster member and complete mission by division of labor and cooperation. LEACH circulates cluster head randomly for distributing energy consumption and fuses the data within the cluster in the cluster head for reducing communication cost, and this technique comprises several rounds. After formatting the clusters, the cluster head broadcast TDMA schedule which indicates data transmission order of cluster members. By this way, each cluster member transmits data only in own transmit slot and in the rest of time slots can go to sleep mode and decrease power consumption. It is the similar way while cluster heads transmit aggregation data to base station. The performance of LEACH counts on evenly deploying cluster head and the number of cluster head at each round. But it can not be guaranteed by selecting cluster head itself.

Because LEACH can not be guaranteed by selecting cluster head itself, LEACHC [52] is proposed that decides cluster head and cluster concerning location information of sensor node and energy from base station.

Banerjee et al. presented an efficient distributed clustering algorithm to create a hierarchical control structure and the set of desired clusters [13]. WSN is viewed as an unweighted connected graph and a cluster is defined as a subset of vertices.

Clustering problem can be viewed as a search problem through a typically NP-hard solution space. In this sense, some researchers have adopted nature-inspired approaches for WSNs.

The hybridization of a Genetic Algorithms (GA) with existing algorithms can always produce a better algorithm than either the GA or the existing algorithms alone [18, 151, 34].

Chia et al. [67] proposed an evolutionary recurrent network which automates the design of recurrent neural/fuzzy networks using a new evolutionary learning algorithm. This new evolutionary learning algorithm is based on a hybrid of genetic algorithm (GA) and particle swarm optimization (PSO), and is thus called HGAPSO. In HGAPSO, individuals in a new generation are created, not only by crossover and mutation operation as in GA, but also by PSO.

In [127], Tillet et al. proposed a Particle Swarm Optimisation (PSO) approach for the same problem. However, the main aim was to reduce an intra-cluster distance by completely ignoring the distance to the sink.

In [63], Ji et al. applied Divided Range Particle Swarm Optimisation (DRPSO) to optimise weighted clustering algorithm (WCA)[27] parameters.

Different approaches to combine PSO with the other evolutionary algorithms have been reported. Robinson et al. in [111] obtained better results by applying PSO first followed by applying GA in their profiled corrugated horn antenna optimization problem. In [76], either particle swarm optimization algorithm, genetic algorithm, or hill climbing search algorithm can be applied to a different sub-population of individuals which each individual is dynamically assigned to according to some pre-designed rules. In [54], ant colony optimization is combined with PSO. A list of best positions found so far is recorded and the neighbourhood best is randomly selected from the list instead of the current neighbourhood best.

Also, non-evolutionary techniques have been incorporated into PSO. In [16], a Cooperative Particle Swarm Optimizer (CPSO) is implemented. The CPSO employs cooperative behaviour to significantly improve the performance of the original PSO algorithm through using multiple swarms to optimize different components of the solution vector cooperatively.

In the self-organization of the WSN, two directions have been paid much attention. The former kind is the coverage-based method [126, 88], which concerns on ensuring the complete sensing coverage with node number as small as possible. Only when one or more operated nodes happen to fail, does the network organization implement once more. It is actually a static method without considering the dynamic of target state. The latter is the distributed collaborative sensing method [77, 143, 144, 148, 156], which constructs an integrated performance index of tracking accuracy and communication cost. By optimizing the performance index online, it achieves a trade off between the energy cost and sensing performance. However it usually requires a cluster head and some cluster members to form a centralized construction. Moreover, such centralized optimization may not be practical because each node has very limited computation ability. Besides this, the priori location information of each node is needed beforehand.

Raluca Marin [86] proposed *Tandem* algorithm which is a context-aware method for spontaneous clustering of wireless sensor nodes. The behaviour of the algorithm is approximated by using Markov chain model. The algorithm allows re-clustering in case of topological or contextual changes. The difference between the derived approximation and the real situation is increasing with the number of groups. This algorithm is valid only for one-hop clusters.

3.7 Summary

This Chapter has investigated the common behaviour of Swarms (Flocks, Herds, and Schools) and the concepts of Swarm Intelligence (SI) in nature.

The interaction between computer science and computer optimization and how this has yielded to new practical solvers for global optimization problems, called metaheuristics is explained.

Genetic Algorithms (GAs) as part of Evolutionary Computations (ECs) is explained showing how this technique can be used as an efficient search algorithm to simulate the adaptive evolution process of natural systems.

On the other hand, Particle Swarm Optimization (PSO) technique is explored with different modified versions and how this optimization technique can be used as a solution for energy efficient mobile WSNs.

Compared with EC methods, PSO does not have as many parameters to tune in order to get acceptable performance. Although PSO has the ability to converge quickly, it tends to wander and slow down as it approaches an optimum. Owing to the premature convergence, it gets stuck quite easily and cannot explore wide enough. This can be problematic for solving multimodal problems where the problems have multiple optimal solutions.

Particle swarms have a unique way of using gradient information to guide their search. A particle moves in a stochastic oscillatory trajectory through the problem space, sampling around relatively optimal local points, while an evolutionary individual searches by changing position through mutation and crossover.

The deployment of SI in WSNs is mentioned, including energy optimization approaches in WSNs, clustering algorithms for Mobile WSNs, and the hybrid approaches between PSO and other Evolutionary Algorithms.

In the next Chapter, the design details of the presented ENAMS algorithm are presented, based on the optimization techniques that are explained in this Chapter.

Chapter 4

ENAMS: Energy Optimization Algorithm for Mobile WSNs

4.1 Introduction

This chapter presents the developed ENAMS algorithm (Energy optimizatioN Algorithm for Mobile Sensor networks) which is based on Evolutionary Computation (EC) and Swarm Intelligence (SI). It is composed of two phases; Phase-1 is designed to divide the sensor nodes into independent clusters by using Genetic Algorithms (GAs) to minimize the overall communication distance between the sensor-nodes and the sink-point. This will decrease the energy consumption for the entire network. Phase-2 is designed to keep the optimum sensors' distribution while the mobile sensor network is directed as a swarm to achieve a given goal. It is based on Particle Swarm Optimization (PSO).

One of the main strengths in the presented system is that the number of clusters within the sensor network is not predefined, this gives more flexibility for the nodes' deployment in the sensor network. Another strength is that sensors' density is not necessary to be uniformly distributed among the clusters, since in some applications constraints, the sensors need to be deployed in different densities depending on the nature of the application domain.

4.2 Design Challenges

The use of clusters for transmitting data to the sink-point enforces the advantages of short transmission distances for most sensor-nodes within the WSN, requiring only a few nodes to transmit far distances.

One of the main challenges in designing ENAMS algorithm is the complexity of finding the optimal number of clusters and the best positions for the cluster-heads. This complexity increases as the number of sensor-nodes increases. For example, to perform an exhausted search of all possible solutions of a sensor network with 100 nodes will require:

$$C_{100}^{1} + C_{100}^{2} + ... + C_{100}^{100} = 2^{100} - 1$$

different combination which is far too large to be handled by normal computer resources. Our target in this research is the high density mobile sensor networks.

The second challenge in the design of ENAMS algorithm is how to keep the clustered topology of the sensor network in the optimised structure during the movement of the mobile sensors. It can be observed that most of the existing clustering algorithms are less suitable for mobile environment. The reasons for that are: The process of electing the cluster-heads based on information from nodes which are multiple hopes away leads to high overhead and slow reaction to topology changes. Also, maintaining complete intra-cluster information is an expensive task which results in a high traffic. Finally, the complexity of the multi-layer clustering algorithms leads to a lot of efforts in building and maintaining the desired structure.

4.3 Phase-1: Distance Optimization using GAs

The design of phase-1 for the presented energy-efficient algorithm (ENAMS) is based on a developed Genetic Algorithms (GAs) to optimize the communication distance of Wireless Sensor Networks in which a large number of sensors are deployed to achieve a given goal. To minimize the energy dissipation, the sensor-nodes are divided into clusters (see Section 2.4.1). This will decrease the communication distances between the sensor-nodes and the sink-point. The relation between the communication distance and the energy dissipation will be explained in more details in the following Section.

4.3.1 Energy Model for Optimization

The recent developments in micro-electro-mechanical systems technology, wireless communications, and digital electronics have enabled the expansion of low-cost, low-power, multifunctional sensor nodes that can be aggregated into a wireless sensor network. Energy constraints are the driving factors in the design of wireless sensor networks, which require low power consumption and energy efficient communication protocols.

Direct transmission networks are very straightforward to design but can be very power-consuming due to the long distances from sensors to the sink-point (Data Collector). Figure 4.1 is an example of WSN with direct transmission where each sensor transmits messages directly to the sink-point.

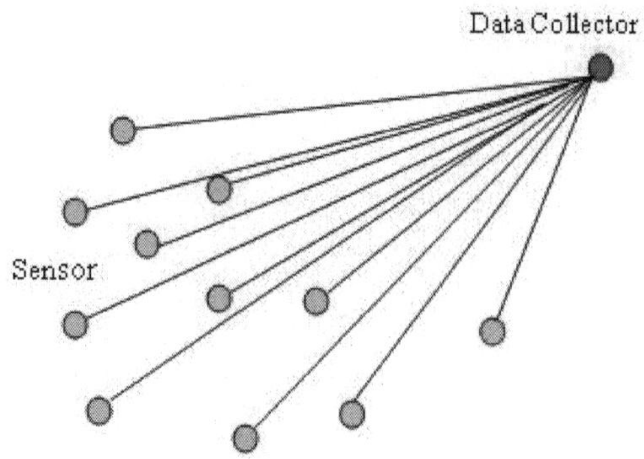

Figure 4.1: Direct transmission example

Alternative designs that shorten or minimize the communication links can decrease the power consumption and extend network lifetime. One of these techniques is to divide the sensor network into clusters. Each cluster usually has one cluster-head which communicates with the sensor nodes that are related to that cluster, and forward the aggregated data to sink-point. Figure 4.2 shows an example of clustered WSN.

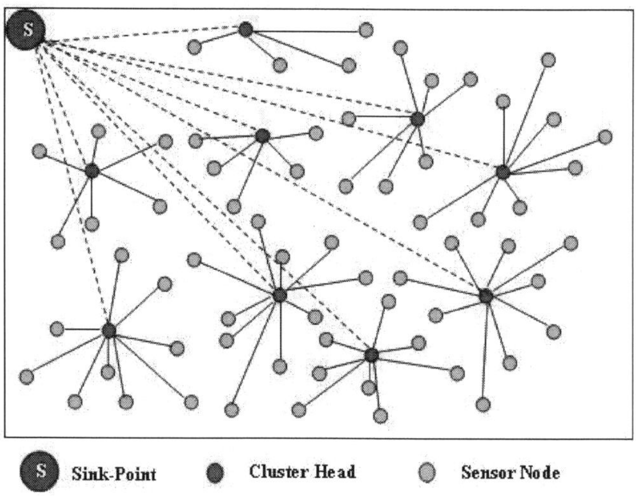

Figure 4.2: Clustered Sensors Network

The important components of each sensor are the data and central processing unit and the radio for communication. The microprocessor used in the processing unit of the sensor's platform should be energy efficient with less energy consumption. The energy dissipation for transmitting *b* bits through distance *d* is shown in Equation 4.1.

$$E_{tx}(b, d) = E_{elec} \times b + E_{amp} \times b \times d^2 \tag{4.1}$$

The energy dissipation in a node to receive b bits of data is shown in Equation 4.2.

$$E_{rx}(b) = E_{elec} \times b \tag{4.2}$$

where E_{elec} is the radio energy dissipation and E_{amp} is the transmition amplifier energy dissipation.

Energy consumption of a wireless sensor node transmitting and receiving data from another node at a distance d can be divided into two main components: Energy used to transmit, receive and amplify data; and energy used for processing the data, mainly by the microcontroller. Leakage current can be as large as a few mA for the microcontroller, and the effect of leakage current can be neglected for higher frequencies and lower supply voltage. Assuming the leakage current as negligible, the total energy loss for the sensor system due to the distance E_{dd} can be calculated according to Figure 4.3 using the following equation:

$$E_{dd} = \left(\sum_{j=1}^{k} \sum_{i=1}^{n_j} (d_{ij}^2 + \frac{D_j^2}{n_j}) \right) \tag{4.3}$$

where D_j is the distance between cluster-heads and the sink-point, d_{ij} is the distance between the sensor-nodes and its related cluster-heads. k represents the number of clusters and n is the total number of sensors in the network.

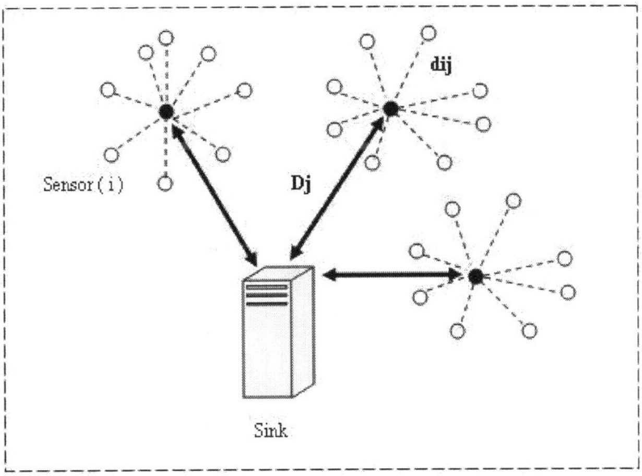

Figure 4.3: Energy Model for distance based Sensor Network

4.3.2 Chromosome Representation

Specifying the appropriate nodes to be the cluster-head for each group of sensor-nodes is critically important for minimizing the distance. In this research we are using binary chromosome representation in which each bit corresponds to one sensor. A "1" means that corresponding sensor is a cluster-head; otherwise, it is a regular node. In Figure 4.4, the individual nodes S1, S4 and S6 are cluster-heads. The remaining nodes are regular nodes. The initial population consists of randomly generated individuals. Each regular node uses a deterministic method to find its nearest cluster-head.

S1	S2	S3	S4	S5	S6	S7	S8
1	0	0	1	0	1	0	0

Figure 4.4: Chromosome representation for cluster-heads and regular nodes

In this research we have developed the basic GA in a way that in case of any cluster-head remain unconnected with any regular sensor then its state should be changed to be a regular node and linked to the nearest cluster-head available in the field. This process will eliminate inefficient clusters to survive. Decreasing the number of clusters will enhance the overall distance optimization of the sensors network. As a result the optimization process will produce more energy efficient topology for the sensor network.

Once cluster-heads are selected, each regular node connects to its nearest cluster-head. Each node in a network is either a cluster-head or a "member" of a cluster-head. Each regular node can only belong to one cluster-head. Cluster-heads collects data from all sensors within its cluster and directly sends the collected data to the sink-point. If a regular node becomes a cluster-head after crossover, all other regular nodes should check if they are closer to this new cluster-head. If so, they switch their membership to the new cluster-head. The new cluster-head is detached from its previous cluster. If a cluster-head becomes a regular node, all of its members must find new cluster-heads.

Each individual in the GA population represents a possible solution to the problem. Finding individuals which are the best suggestions to our problem and combine these individuals into new individuals is an important stage of the evolutionary process. Using this method repeatedly, the population should evolve good solutions. Crossover and mutation provide exploration, compared with the exploitation provided by selection. The effectiveness of GA depends on the trade-off between exploitation and exploration [117].

Crossover: The crossover operation takes place between two consecutive individuals with probability specified by crossover rate. These two individuals exchange portions that are separated by the crossover point. In the developed ENAMS algorithm we have used one-point crossover type. Figure 4.5 shows an example of crossover. After crossover, two offspring are created as shown in Figure 4.6.

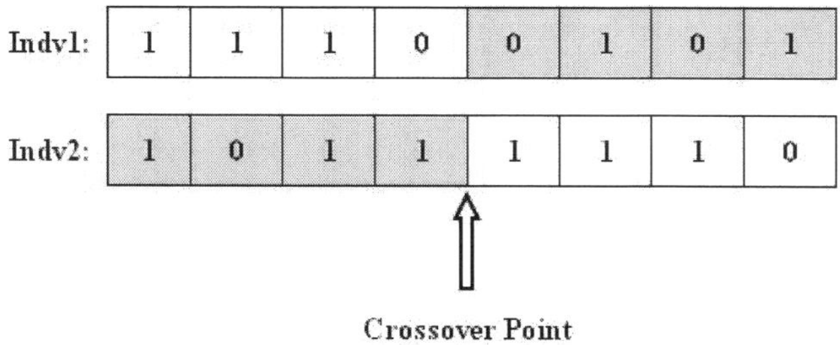

Figure 4.5: Example of Crossover

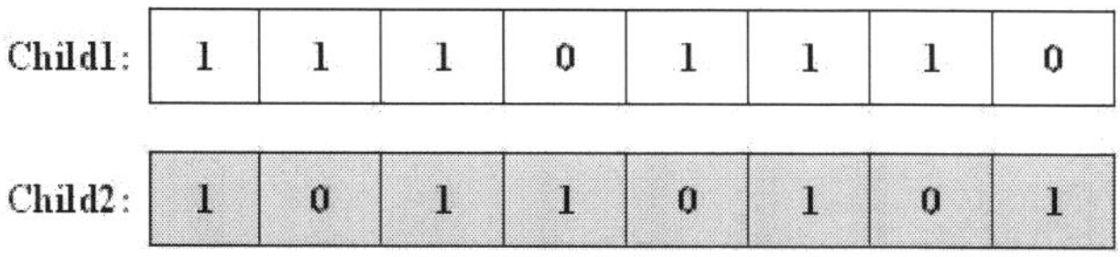

Figure 4.6: Two offspring created by Crossover

Mutation: The mutation operator is applied to each bit of an individual with a probability of mutation rate. When applied, a bit whose value is 0 is mutated into 1 and vice versa. An example of mutation shown in Figure 4.7.

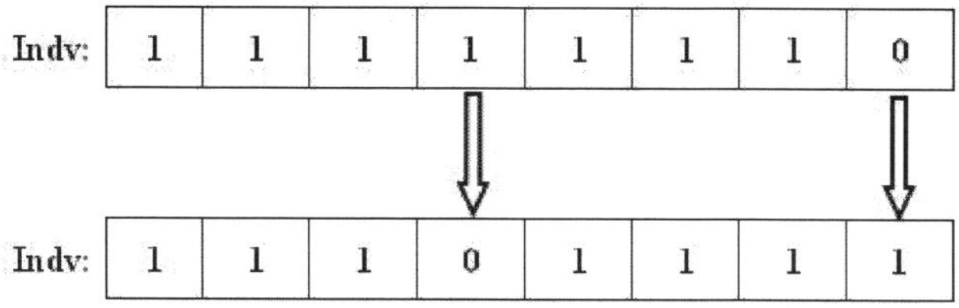

Figure 4.7: Example of Mutation

4.3.3 Distance - Clusters Rule

The total transmission distance is the main factor we need to minimize. In addition, the number of cluster heads can factor into the fitness function. In designing our fitness function required for GAs process, we are considering that; given the same distance, fewer cluster heads result in greater energy efficiency as cluster heads drain more power than non-cluster-heads.

Thus, each individual is evaluated by the following combined fitness components:

$$Fitness = w \times (D - distance_i) + (1 - w) \times (N - H_i) \quad (4.4)$$

where D is the total distance of all nodes to the sink, $distance_i$ is the sum of the distances from regular nodes to cluster-heads plus the sum of the distances from all cluster-heads to the sink; H_i is the number of cluster-heads; N is the total number of nodes; and w is a predefined weight. The value of w is between 0 and 1, and it is application-dependent. It indicates which factor is more important to be considered: distance or the cost incurred by cluster-heads.

At one extreme, if $w = 1$, we optimize the network only based on the communication distance. If $w = 0$, only the number of cluster heads is considered. Except for $distance_i$ and H_i, all other parameters are fixed values in a given topology. The shorter the distance, or the lower the number of cluster-heads, the higher the fitness value of an individual is. ENAMS algorithm tries to maximize the fitness value to find a good solution. The developed Phase-1 of ENAMS algorithm is shown in Algorithm 2. This algorithm appears in our publication [97].

```
Initialization: Generate random population of n chromosomes
while the stop condition is not satisfied do
    if cluster-head not connected to any sensor-node then
        change cluster-head state into regular sensor;
        find the nearest cluster-head to be connected with;
    end
    Evaluate the fitness g(x) of each chromosome x in the population;
    while the new population is not complete do
        Selection: Select two parent chromosomes from a population
        according to their fitness
        Crossover: With a crossover probability, crossover the parents
        to form a new offspring (children);
        Mutation: With a mutation probability mutate new offspring;
        Accepting: Place new offspring in a new population;
    end
    Replace: Use new generated population for further runs;
end
Return: the best solution of the current population;
```

Algorithm 2: Phase-1 of ENAMS Algorithm

4.4 Phase-2: Distance Management Using SI

The second part of ENAMS algorithm is designed to provide the distance management by using Particle Swarm Optimization (PSO) which makes the wireless sensor network self organized while the sensors are moving on a swarm bases. In PSO, the potential solutions are called particles, fly through the problem space by following the current optimum particles. The particles are initialised randomly. Each particle will have a fitness value, which will be evaluated by the fitness function to be optimised in each generation. Each particle knows its best position *pbest* and the best position so far among the entire group of particles *gbest*. The particle will have velocities, which direct the flying of the particle. In each generation the velocity and the position of the particle will be updated. The velocity and the position update equations are given below as (4.5) and (4.6) respectively. These equations were described previously with more details in Section (3.5.2).

$$v_i^{k+1} = wv_i^k + c_1rand_1 \times (pbest_i - s_i^k) + c_2rand_2 \times (gbest - s_i^k) \tag{4.5}$$

$$x_i^{k+1} = x_i^k + v_i^k{+}1 \tag{4.6}$$

The parameters used in Equations (4.5) and (4.6) are described in Table 4.1.

4.4.1 Fitness Function for PSO

Referring to Equation (4.3), we can conclude that by reducing the distance from a node to the cluster-head and the cluster-head to the sink-point we can minimise the energy dissipation in a sensor network. In our system, we cluster the nodes taking into consideration that each node can transmit or receive data from all other nodes.

Table 4.1: The parameters for PSO velocity and position update

Parameter	Description
v_i^k	velocity of particle i at iteration k
w	inertia weight
v_i^{k+1}	velocity of particle i at iteration $k + 1$
c_j	acceleration coefficients j=1,2
$rand_i$	random number between 0 and 1 i=1,2
s_i^k	current position of particle i at iteration k
$pbest_i$	best position of particle i
$gbest$	best position so far among the entire group of particles
x_i^{k+1}	position of the particle i at iteration $k + 1$

Thus, nodes considered in this network do not have transmission range constraint. Sensors are clustered using entirely distance based Equation (4.3). Here the number of clusters is produced from the former phase of our algorithm by GA part, hence the nodes are distributed within a given number of clusters 'k'. The fitness function for this phase of our algorithm is shown in Equation (4.7).

$$Fitness = min\left(\sum_{j=1}^{k}\sum_{i=1}^{n_j}(d_{ij}^2 + \frac{D_j^2}{n_j})\right) \tag{4.7}$$

where,

$\sum_{j=1}^{k}(n_j + k) = N.$

N is the total number of nodes in the network. The pseudo code for phase-2 of ENAMS algorithm is shown in Algorithm (3).

```
PSO Initialization: Assume the initial population is the best solution
generated by the previous stage of GAs;
while the stop condition is not satisfied do
    Evaluate the fitness value for each particle's position in the
    swarm;
    if fitness(p) better than fitness(pbest) then
        pbest = p;
        Set best of pbest as gbest;
    end
    Update the particles' velocity v_i^k+1;
    Update the particles' position x_i^k+1;
end
```

Algorithm 3: Phase-2 of ENAMS Algorithm

4.5 ENAMS Algorithm: The Hybrid Approach

Any WSN is deeply involved in and related to the monitored environment, and any change occurring to the surroundings will significantly influence its performance; nevertheless, the network must be able to tolerate and 'survive' any change by implementing proper reactions and adaptation mechanisms sustaining communications for both sensed data and commands.

This section describes the complete ENAMS algorithm by combining phase-1 and phase-2 which are described in Sections (4.3) and (4.4) respectively. The produced hybrid algorithm which is based on Evolutionary

Computation and Swarm Intelligence is an efficient algorithm for energy optimization of mobile wireless sensor networks.

To obey the self-working paradigm, WSN protocols should be designed with strong attention to both device coordination and redundancy exploitation issues, both of which might have to cope with the network member resource heterogeneity. A vision to reach this autonomy is through the concept of self-organization, which is defined in [23] as "the spontaneous creation of a globally coherent pattern out of local interactions". Local interactions will be probably based on local rules to achieve a global goal. Note that the local rules assigned to each sensor may be different depending on its hardware characteristics, node location, traffic pattern, security, and other attributes associated with the application. The ultimate goal of these local rules is to design a self-organizing WSN.

Figure 4.8 combines Algorithms (2) and (3), showing the flow of ENAMS phases to achieve the energy optimization for a mobile WSN.

4.6 Summary

In this chapter, the design of ENAMS algorithm is presented, in two phases; Phase-1 is based on Genetic Algorithms (GAs) with some enhancements to divide the sensor nodes into independent clusters to minimize the overall communication distance between the sensor-nodes and the sink-point for the entire network. Each node in a network is either a cluster-head or a "member" of a cluster-head. Each regular node can only belong to one cluster-head. Cluster-heads collect data from all sensors within their cluster and directly send the collected data to the sink-point. If a regular node becomes a cluster-head after crossover, all other regular nodes should check if they are closer to this new cluster-head. If so, they switch their membership to the new cluster-head. The new cluster-head is detached from its previous cluster. If a cluster-head becomes a regular node, all of its members must find new cluster-head.

Phase-2 is based on Swarm Intelligence (SI) which is designed to keep the optimum sensors' distribution while the mobile sensors are directed as a swarm to achieve a given goal.

In the next Chapter, the design of a simulation system is presented to analyse and evaluate the ENAMS algorithm.

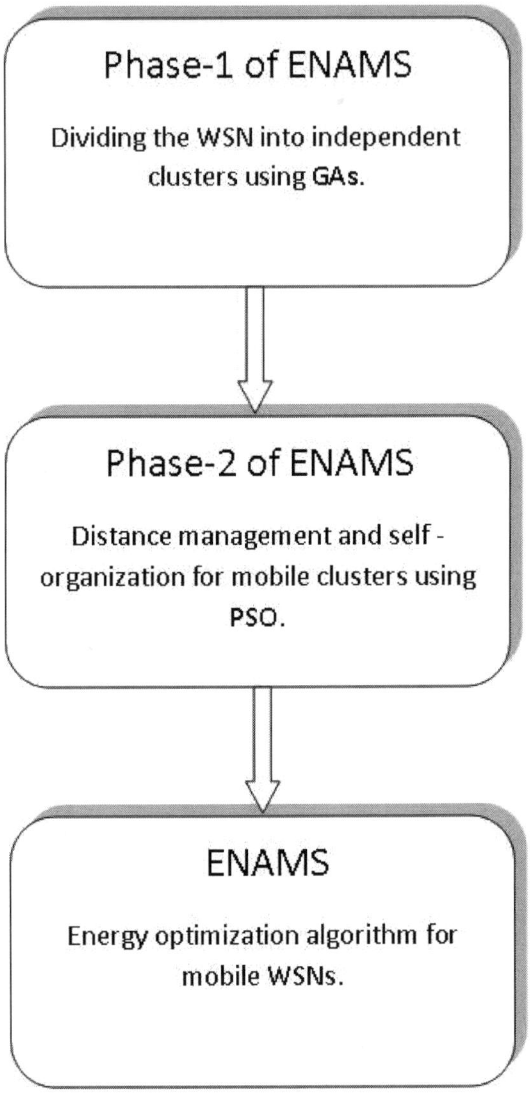

Figure 4.8: Phases flow of ENAMS Algorithm

Chapter 5

Simulation

5.1 Introduction

This chapter presents the software implementation of the presented ENAMS algorithm which is designed for energy optimization of mobile WSNs by using Evolutionary Computation and Swarm Intelligence.

The first phase of the algorithm is to divide the network into clusters by using GAs, where the number of clusters is not predefined and number of sensor-nodes within each cluster is not necessary to be the same. This makes ENAMS algorithm more flexible in terms of the designed network topology which can cover a wide range of applications.

The second phase of the algorithm enabling the sensors to move as a swarm using PSO while keeping the optimum distances between the sensor-nodes and their related cluster-head, avoiding any unnecessary movements.

5.2 Operational Specifications for Simulation

To verify the goals of the presented ENAMS algorithm, we have designed a 2-D simulation environment for the wireless sensor network having randomly generated sensor-nodes to be considered as the initial population for the GAs process. We used Java-Applet to simulate the experiments of 80 nodes considering different sink positions to cover a variety of applications' specifications. The tuning parameters used for GAs in the simulated experiments are given in Table 5.1.

Table 5.1: The GA parameters settings

Parameter	Value
Population size	80
Selection type	Proportional
Crossover rate	0.7
Crossover type	one point

Mutation rate	0.005
Generation size	1000

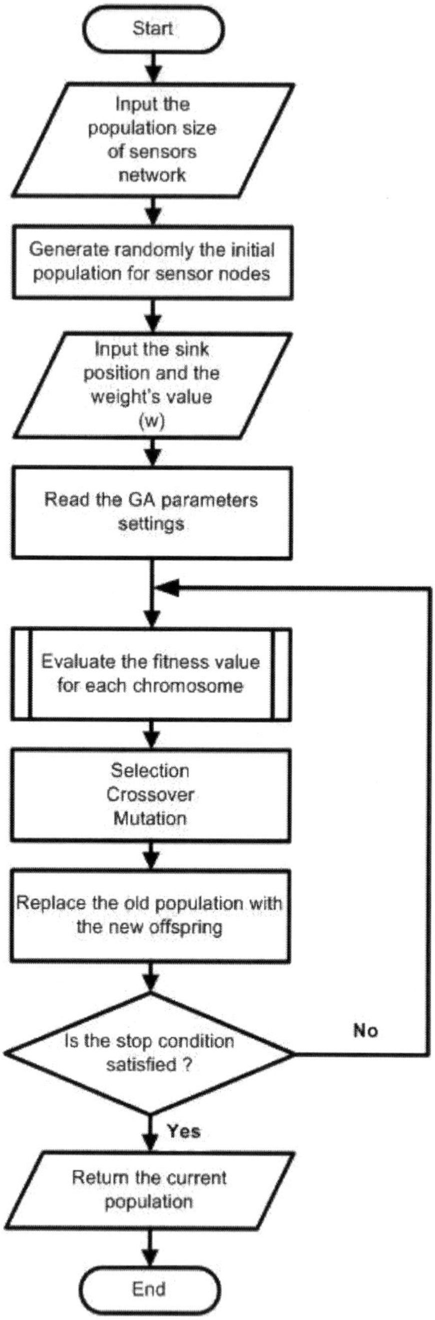

Figure 5.1: Flowchart for Part-1 of ENAMS simulation system

Figure 5.1 shows the flowchart for phase-1 of ENAMS algorithm at which the Ad hoc WSN is clustered by using GAs. For more details about the Java coding for implementing the simulator, refer to Appendix (A). The implementation of these simulation experiments appears in our publication [95].

5.3 Evolving Clustered WSN Using GAs

Among many experiments achieved to divide the WSN into K-clusters by using GAs with a tuning parameters such that described in the previous section, We are exploring the following cases:

5.3.1 Experiment-1: WSN with Sink located at (0,0)

This experiment demonstrates the case when the sink point is located at (0,0) (i.e. the upper left corner) and the value of the predefined weight w is set (1.0) (see Section 4.3.3). This network distribution is suitable when the application environment is inhospitable, which will be not safe to allocate the sink-point (i.e. data collector) within the field area, like some military applications or earthquake observations. see Figure 5.2. Our observation in this experiment is that, when a single sensor node located near to the sink point, that node itself becomes a cluster-head and sends the data directly to the sink. Also, for the nodes which are near the sink are more likely become cluster-heads than those faraway from it.

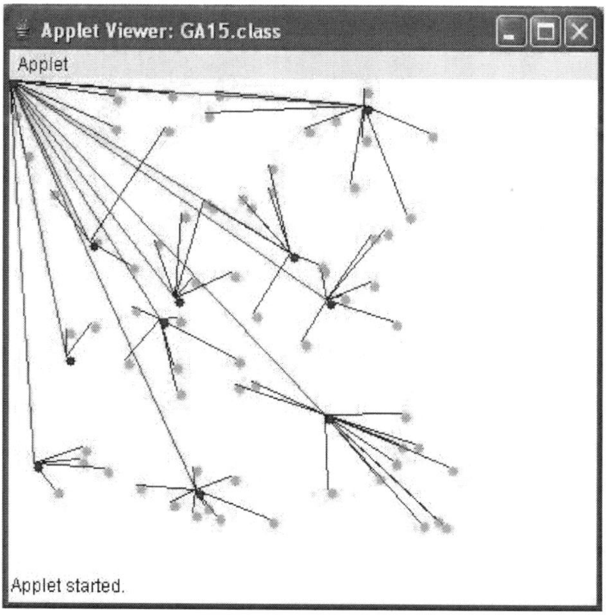

Figure 5.2: Clustered network when sink point at (0,0)

5.3.2 Experiment-2: WSN with Sink located at (100,100)

This experiment demonstrates the case when the sink point is located near the centre of the network, for example at the point (100,100) and the value of w set to (0.8). This network distribution is more suitable when the sensor nodes are distributed around a centralized safe area where the sink-point can receive the data in a wider circular range and from different directions. For example the Mobile networks, see Figure 5.3. In the majority of the outcomes for this experiment, we found that more cluster-heads are needed than the previous experiment. This is due to the sink location. This behavior is expected because when the sink point located at the centre, more density of sensor nodes is available around it. As a result, more cluster-heads tends to be distributed around the sink point.

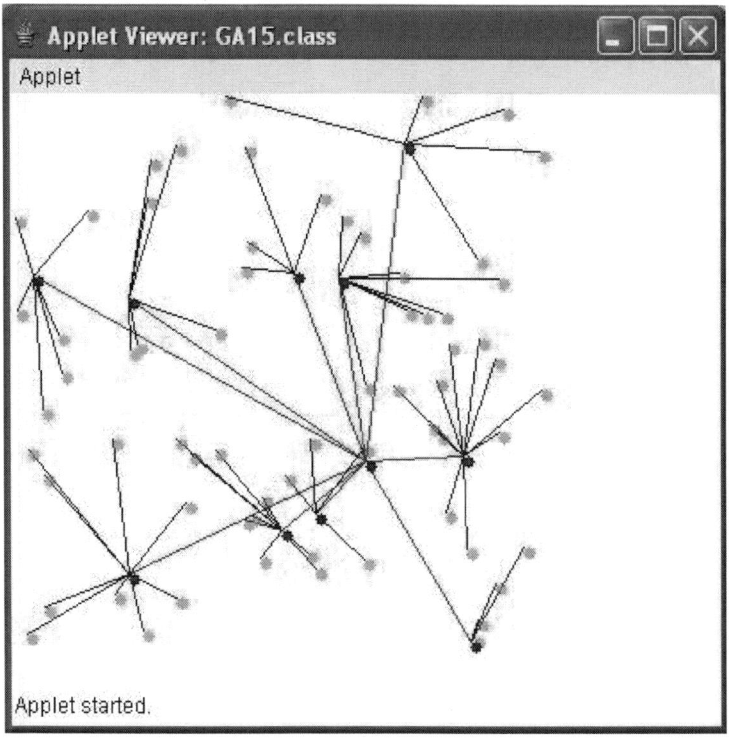

Figure 5.3: Clustered network when sink point at (100,100)

5.3.3 Experiment-3: WSN with Sink located at (0,0) and the predefined weight (w=0)

This experiment describes the situation when the number of cluster-heads is only considered in the fitness function, that is when the value of the predefined weight w is set to (0.0). Although this is not realistic in our research-problem, but it verifies the effectiveness of ENAMS algorithm because, as expected, the optimal number of heads is equal to 1. See Figure 5.4.

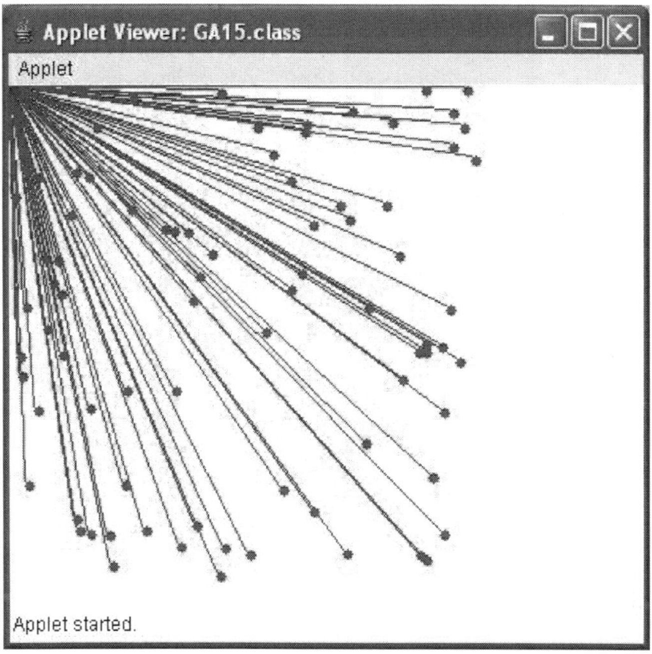

Figure 5.4: Clustered network when w=0

5.3.4 Scalability

The ability to maintain performance characteristics irrespective of the size of the network is referred to as *scalability* [69]. Hundreds or thousands of the nodes can be deployed in a sensor network, since the cost of the sensors recently become relatively low. With WSNs potentially consisting of thousands of nodes, scalability is an evidently indispensable requirement.

It is very important to test the scalability of the designed optimization algorithm. In our experiments, we have increased the number of sensor-nodes from 80,160, to 1280, see Figure 5.5.

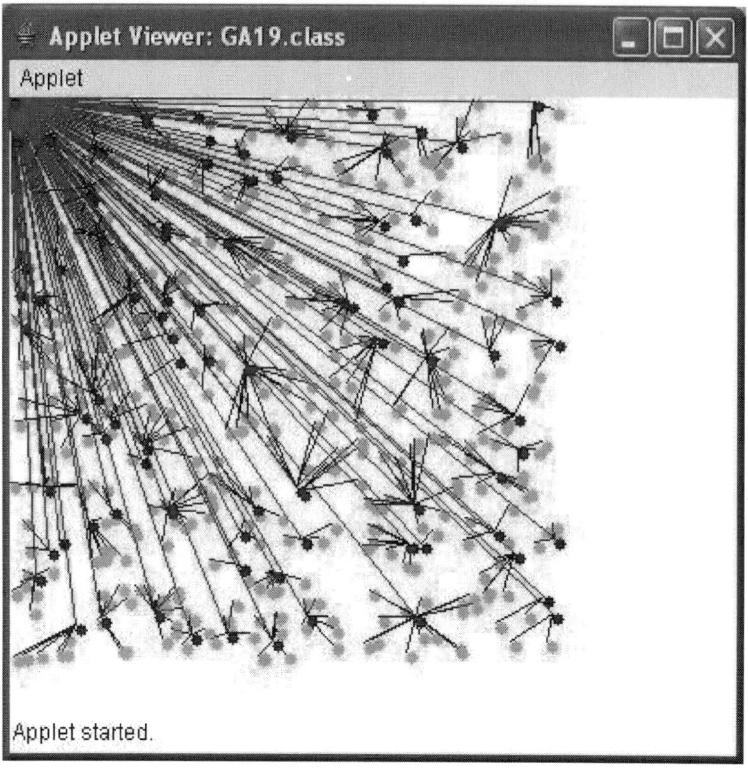

Figure 5.5: Large scale clustered WSN with 1280 sensor nodes

Table(5.2) illustrates some initial test results when the sink-point is assumed to be at point (0,0). As an average value, the distance is reduced by 84% as compared with the distance when direct transmission is used.

Table 5.2: Test results for different problem size

No. Nodes	Total distance without clustering	Total distance with clustering	Distance decreased
80	16945	4581	73.96%
160	36301	6541	81.98%
320	71687	9929	86.15%
640	148700	20125	86.64%
1280	293244	20221	93.10%

This percentage will slightly increase as the number of nodes increases because, as more nodes will be deployed in the network with denser distribution, this will result in more efficient cluster optimization.

5.4 Fitness Value and Number of Clusters Over Generations

Analysis of the fitness values observed for most of our experimentations, we can see that the fitness value is greatly enhanced after 100 generations due to the selection of the best fitness chromosomes to be used in the next generation. Figure 5.6 shows the maximum fitness value reached over generations.

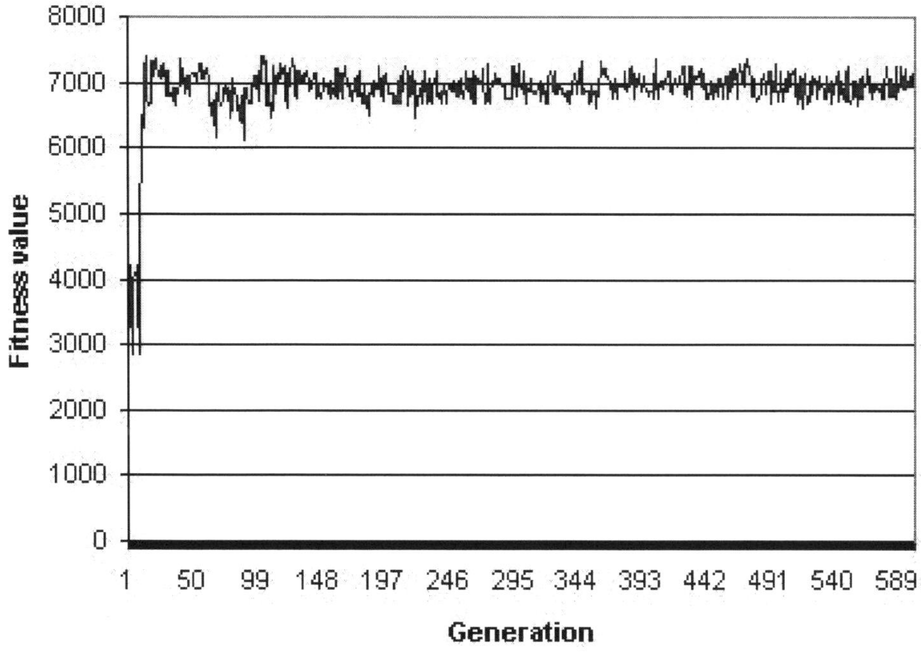

Figure 5.6: Fitness values over generations

In Figure 5.7, number of cluster heads decreases over generations to reach around 25% from the overall number of nodes in the network. This verifies the effectiveness of our algorithm because, as expected, the total distance will be minimized as the number of heads decreases. This percentage value may vary if the sensor nodes are unevenly distributed over the network field.

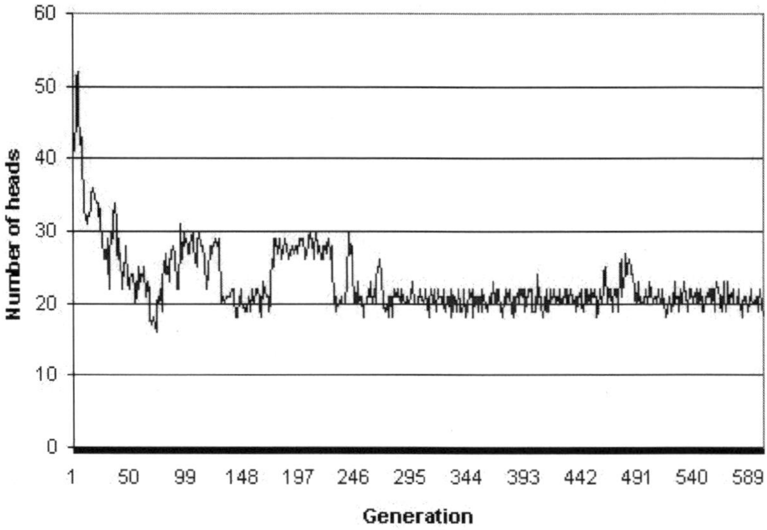

Figure 5.7: Number of cluster heads over generations

5.5 Mobile Clustered WSN Using PSO

Referring to equations (4.5) and (4.6) explained in the previous chapter, the particles' velocities are continuously adjusted over generations enabling the swarm to move within the search space keeping the optimum distribution. We have taken the advantages of this criterion to enable the sensor nodes of the clustered Wireless Sensor Network to be mobile sensors moving together as swarms throughout the generations of PSO process. The fitness function used for this part of ENAMS algorithm is shown in Section (4.4.1). The maximum number of generations we were running was 1000. The parameters used in the simulations are tabulated in Table (5.3). Figure 5.8 shows the flowchart for phase-2 of ENAMS algorithm which is responsible of avoiding the mobile sensor nodes to do any unnecessary movements by achieving self-organization while they are moving as swarms using PSO.

Table 5.3: The PSO Parameters settings

Parameter	Range
Population size	80
MAXITER	1000
v_{max}	100
x_{max}	100

v range	0-100
x range	0-100

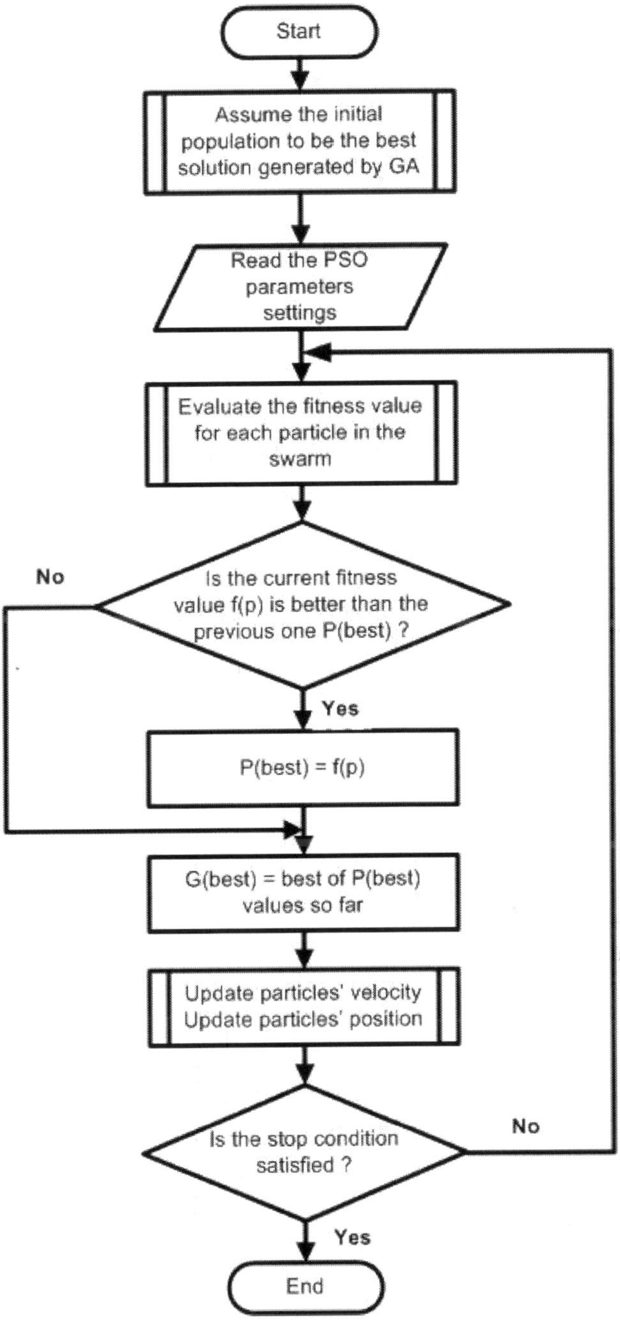

Figure 5.8: Flowchart for Part-2 of ENAMS simulation system

In this simulation, we observed the performance in terms of quality of the average optimum value for 10 trials to the **PSO-TVIW** and **PSO-SSM** models which are described in Section 3.5.5 earlier. For both simulations we use the same set of nodes. We have chose these two methods for the following reasons;

The **PSO-SSM** model is the only model which has the ability to stop particles from moving beyond the boundary of the problem space, that is under the influence of the momentum factor (*mc*) in it.

The **PSO-TVIW** model is almost similar to the basic PSO algorithm with just the inertia weight varying with time from 0.9 to 0.4.

From the graph shown in Figure 5.9 we can conclude that **PSO-TVIW** convergence is slower as compared to the **PSO-SSM** algorithm. This was due to constant acceleration co-efficients used in this model which affects the rate of convergence.

Snapshots for the mobile swarmed sensor-nodes are shown in Figure 5.10. Figure 5.10-a shows the initial distribution for sensor-nodes which is produced by GAs from the previous phase of ENAMS algorithm. It can be observed from this distribution that the WSN is clustered into 4-clusters, each one represents a swarm to be directed and controlled by the PSO when it will start running in the second phase of ENAMS. During PSO phase, clusters will be self-organized while they are moving within the experimentation boundaries. This will avoid the mobile sensors to make any unnecessary movements to reserve the energy and enlarge the lifetime for each sensor.

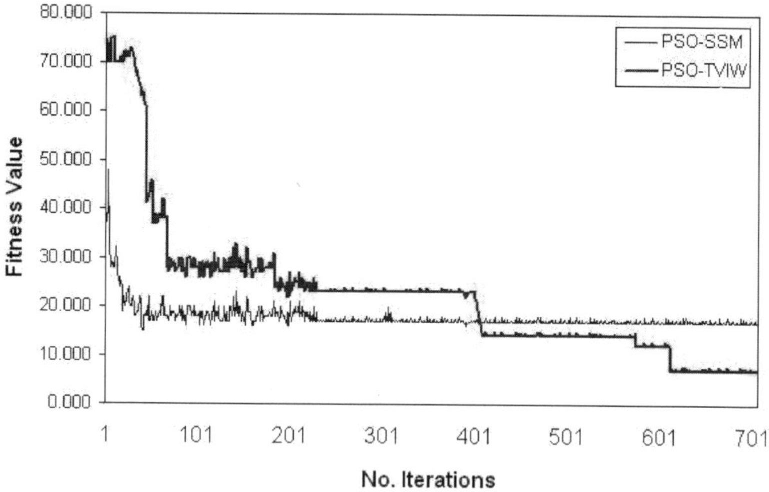

Figure 5.9: Convergence for the PSO-SSM and PSO-TVIW Models

It is clear from the screen shots shown in Figure 5.10 - b, c, d, e and f respectively, that the mobile sensors in each cluster keep adjusting their positions during the movements to keep the distances between the sensor-nodes as much as possible the same as it was in the initial distribution. This work appears in our publication [96].

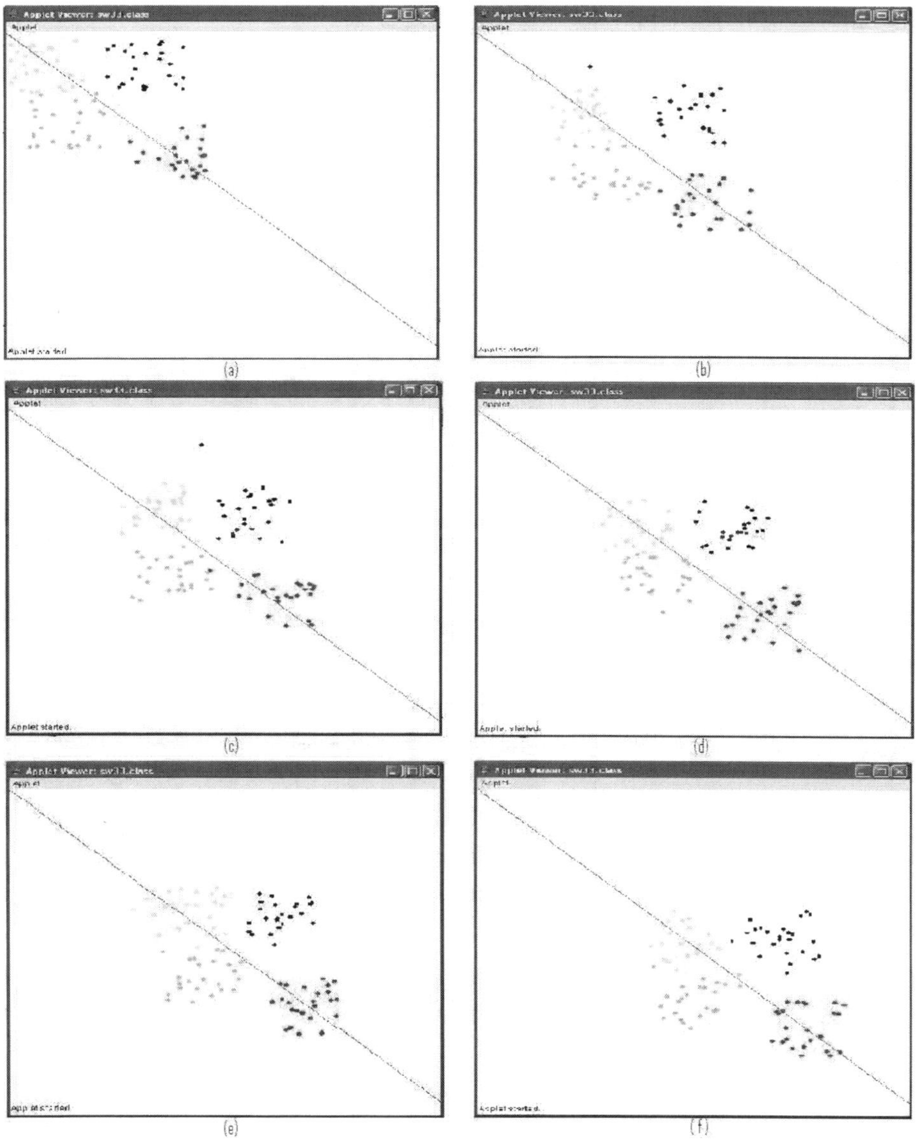

Figure 5.10: Snapshots of swarmed WSN with 4 clusters crossing the problem space

5.6 Summary

In this Chapter, the simulation of ENAMS algorithm is described along with the operational specifications for the experimentation. Among many experiments achieved, three main cases are emphasized. Each case demonstrates the algorithm outcomes in response to the sink-point location and the value of the predefined weight in the fitness function.

The scalability of sensors in the WSN is investigated by increasing the network size from 80,160, to 1280 nodes. The optimization outcomes are also discussed based on screen shots taken from the simulation system.

In order to prove the portability of ENAMS algorithm from the simulation into physical environment, the next Chapter will show the hardware implementation of the algorithm using swarmed Robots.

Chapter 6

Hardware Implementation: Multi-Robot based Simulation

6.1 Introduction

This chapter shows the implementation of ENAMS algorithm to prove it's portability from the simulation environment to a physical swarm of mobile sensors, using a multiple robot system. Since it is likely that any simulator will require physical implementation, we show how this can be achieved. Therefore, this chapter discuss the operational specifications for how the presented ENAMS algorithm would work in the real world on a physical mobile sensor network; i.e. robots.

This chapter is organised as follows:

- The hardware description; the physical specifications of the robots used for this case study is presented in Section 6.2.1
- The communication properties considered, simple definitions are presented in Section 6.3
- The experiments description and results are presented in Section 6.4

6.2 Operational Specifications

6.2.1 Hardware Specifications

LEGO-NXT Mindstorms robots, shown in Figure 6.1, were used as mobile sensors platforms to implement the ENAMS algorithm. This type of robots is selected because it meets our assumptions for the sensors platform to be energy limited. Each robot can communicate with maximum of three other robots at a time.

The technical details of the Lego-NXT Mindstorms robot are as follows: Input/output ports are similar to RJ12 connectors for sensors and motors. It contains four input ports which read the sensors' activities like; Light sensor, Sound sensor, Ultrasound sensor, and Touch sensor. Additionally, It has three output ports which are usually used to drive the three servo motors: A, B and C. Each motor has a built-in rotation sensor. This lets us control the robot's movement precisely. The rotation sensor measures motor rotations in degrees or full rotations with accuracy of +/- one degree. The main processing unit which is usually called (Brick) has the following specification:

- A 32-bit ARM7 microcontroller with a clock frequency of 48MHz

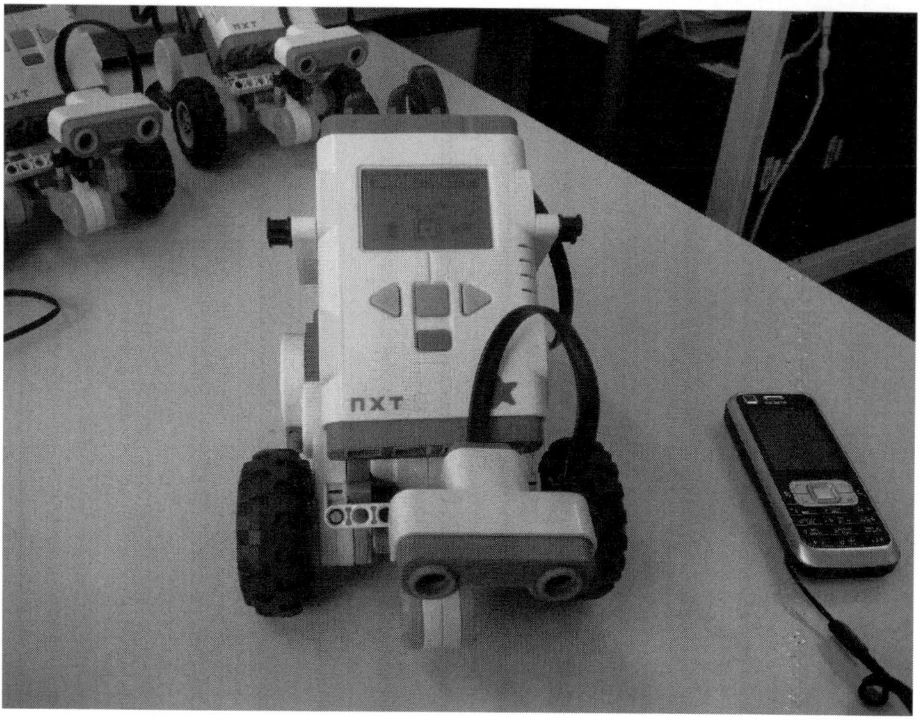

Figure 6.1: LEGO-NXT Mindstorms robot

- Supports Bluetooth communication (Bluetooth Class II V 2.0 compliant)
- 1 USB 2.0 port (12 Mbit/s)
- 256 KB of Flash Memory
- 64 KB of RAM
- 8-bit Atmel AVR microcontroller with a clock frequency of 4MHz
- 4 KB of Flash Memory
- 512 Bytes of RAM
- Loudspeaker 8 kHz sound quality
- The energy source for the robot is six batteries of 1.5 volt AA type

Ultrasonic Sensor:

This sensor gives the robot the ability of vision. By using this sensor, the robot can detect objects and avoid obstacles. This sensor is able to measure the distances from 0 to 255 centimetres with a precision of +/- 3 cm. Large size objects with hard surfaces return the best readings. Objects made of soft fabric or those are curved (like a ball) or very thin can be difficult for the sensor to detect. Also, two or more Ultrasonic sensors operating in the same room may interfere with each other's readings.

6.2.2 Software Specifications

The Lego-NXT Mindstorms robot can be programmed using the **NXT-G** graphical programming environment developed by National Instruments for LEGO robots. Writing an NXT-G program is very much like creating a flowchart. You write a program by dragging icons (code blocks) that describe different behaviours, e.g., turn motor A on at 75 percent of full power, and connect them with lines to describe the program behaviour. Using a variety of code blocks, you can control motors, introduce delays, play sounds and direct the flow of your code according to the state of sensors and timers, etc.

ROBOLAB is another graphical environment which can be used to program the Lego-NXT Mindstorms. It was originally developed by Tufts University for the first generation of LEGO Mindstorms RCX microprocessor. It was extensively enhanced and revised to support both the RCX and the second-generation NXT.

The **ROBOTC** solution allows the NXT to be programmed using the industry-standard C language. It was developed by the Robotics Academy at Carnegie Mellon University and can be obtained from the LEGO Education Group or directly from the Robotics Academy at www.robotc.net. Both of the graphical programming solutions had drag-and-drop capabilities for the code blocks. ROBOTC has a similar capability, but with it, you drag and drop text.

NXJ is a JAVA implementation for the NXT. It is standard JAVA but with a much smaller Class library. The standard Class library is far too large for the total 256K bytes of memory on the NXT. NXJ programs are written and compiled on the PC. The compiled programs are then transferred to the NXT where they can be executed.

We have developed our programs for the experimentation by using NXT-G programming environment because it is easy to be implemented and the software is already supplied with the LEGO kit. For more details about the designed programs for this chapter, please refer to Appendix (B).

6.3 Network Protocol Specification

In order to put the developed algorithm described in Chapter 4, into practice with real robots, we had to consider some network protocols and definitions including the network settings specifications. The communication properties of multi-robot systems can be divided into three categories:

- Implicit Communication
- State Communication
- Explicit Communication

The explicit communication is most suitable to our experimental platform model because we are using Bluetooth broadcasting as a communication media between the master Robot and other slaves Robots. The topology of sensors is single-hope star topology. This type of multi-robot communication is described in the following section.

6.3.1 Explicit Communication

Explicit communication is the intentional transmission and reception of information. It is usually achieved with the help of an underlying communication mechanism such as 802.11 wireless Ethernet, infrared serial, or more recently, Bluetooth. As such, it requires special communication hardware.

Explicit communication in multi-robot systems commonly uses broadcasting or unicasting for communication. A robot might use broadcasting to announce its location to the whole system, or might use unicasting to communicate with another robot right in front of it. The topology used in a multi-robot system ranges from a complete graph, to a hierarchical (tree) based structure. An example of this is a system that consists of workers and leaders, where each leader is in charge of several workers, who can only communicate with their specific leader.

One of the more interesting ideas in explicit communication in multi-robot systems is *abstract* communication versus *situational* communication as described in [68]. In abstract communication, the content of a message is assumed to have all the meaning. For example, one robot R1 may send a message to another robot R2 containing "Go to location x". Robot R2 would then be able to go to location x. In situational communication, the message itself, as well as the message content, has meaning. For example, if R1 sends "move towards me 5 units" R2 is able to determine what it should do from the message content, as well as the localization information from the message itself and information it has about the position of R1. This concept is particularly powerful in situations where a leader (or other landmark) directs a team of robots. For example, a command "everyone, move in closer" is now possible without the leader knowing everyone's position.

Properties of Explicit Communication

- Interaction distance: determined by underlying communication technology.
- Interaction explicitness: both the sender and receiver(s) intend to participate in communication, therefore interaction is explicit.
- Interaction simultaneity: interaction is instantaneous. A robot must be receiving when another is sending.

Benefits of Explicit Communication

- Ease of use. Just plug communication devices into robots, and they're ready to send and receive information.
- The ability to simulate other communication techniques using explicit communication. For example, in [11] Balsh and Arkin use a light to transmit a robot's state, effectively simulating state communication.

Limitations of Explicit Communication

- Dependency on separate communication mechanisms and infrastructures.
- Reliability and robustness limitations due to unreliable underlying communication hardware.

6.4 Experimentation

The setup of the experimentation field is prepared inside the Robotics lab of De Montfort University/Faculty of Technology, which is shown in Figure 6.2. The dimensions of the experiments field is (2.5 x 2.5) meter. In our experiments, the swarm communications are carried out by using Bluetooth, whilst the collision detection is obtained by the Ultrasonic sensors which are mounted on each Robot. The maximum number of communication channels that can be established by the LEGO-NXT Mindstorms Robot with other Robots is three. For the experiments, a cluster-head-robot R1 is (master) and two cluster-member-robots, R2 and R3, will act as a swarm moving in the work space.

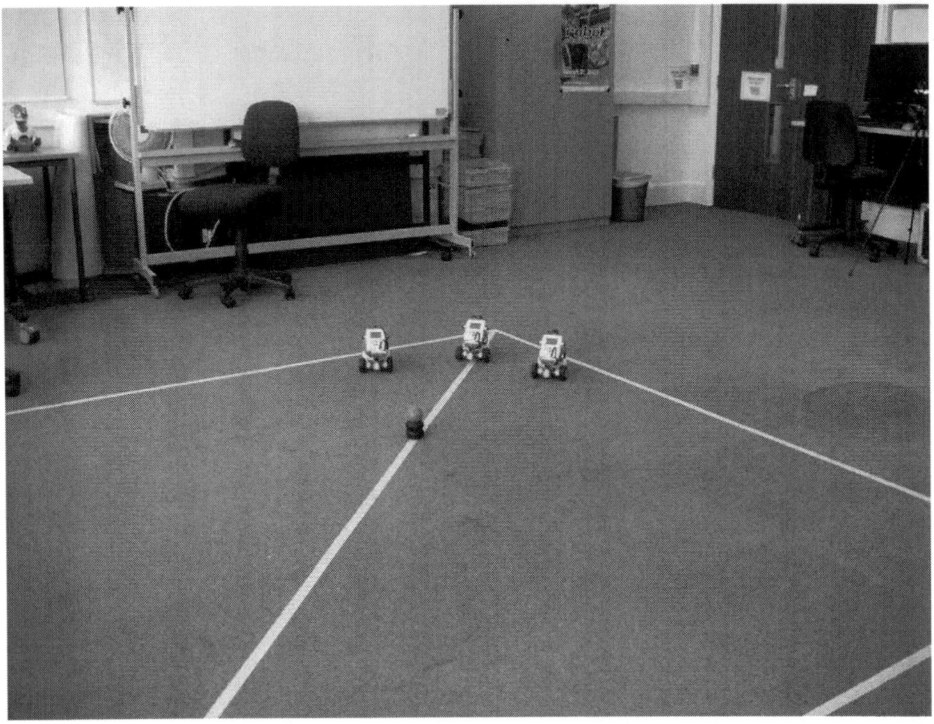

Figure 6.2: Experimentation setup

The cluster-head-robot broadcasts the new positions (direction and speed) for each cluster-member-robot via a distinct Bluetooth channel. Different mailbox numbers should be specified to the left and right motor of each robot to avoid information overlap.

The experiments aims at testing the following:

- Can the swarm of Robots move as a group avoiding each other as well as other obstacles while keeping the optimum deployment structure?
- Is the master Robot (representing the cluster-head) able to communicate with other Robots whilst they are in motion?

6.4.1 Experiment-1: Navigation of Swarmed Robots

Purpose: Navigation of swarmed robots by applying different power values supplied to the robot's motors. The power value can be adjusted in the setting options of the NXT-Robot. As the power value increases the speed of the driving wheels will be higher, keeping in mind that we have to manage the limited energy stored in the Robot's battery and to utilise this energy in an optimum way. By measuring the time required to reach a predefined target location in the experiment field, we can have an indication for the required power value to be specified in the setting of each Robot prior to each mission proposed to be assigned to the swarm of Robots.

Measurements: The time required for the swarmed robots to reach a predefined point in the experiment field.

Results: The Robots are moving as a swarm with continuous interaction between the cluster-head-robot and cluster-member-robots.

The experiment is designed as follows:

The Robots shown in Figure 6.3 are deployed to form a cluster of mobile sensors having a cluster-head Robot R1 with two cluster-members Robots R2 and R3. The experiment starts by establishing a Bluetooth connection among the Robots by assigning different name for each Robot. When the cluster-head Robot (R1) start moving forward across the diagonal of the rectangle field, the other two Robots (R2) and (R3) will combine (R1) keeping the same structure until they reach the end of the diagonal. We have repeated this experiment five times, each with different power value that applied to the motors. Table 6.3 shows the measured time for each power value specified in each trial. This measure will be useful during the planning phase, to estimate the time required for the swarmed Robots to achieve a given goal in a specified mission.

Table 6.1: Motor's power verses time required to reach a target point

Motor Power %	Time (sec)
20	56
40	26
60	17
80	11
100	8

Figure 6.3: Cluster of three Robots

6.4.2 Experiment-2: Swarmed Robots starting from optimum positions

Purpose: Swarmed Robots starting from optimum positions to reach a pre-specified point maintaining the swarm structure. The optimum positions for the Robots are evolved by phase-1 of ENAMS algorithm. In this experiment the Robots are forming a swarm and should move keeping the optimum structure until reaching the target point in the experimentation field.

Measurements: The distances between the cluster-head-robot and the member-robots at the final navigation point, to be within the permitted range.

Results: The final robots' distribution should keep the optimum distances.

The Robots shown in Figure 6.4-a are deployed to form a swarm with three mobile Robots. The initial distances between the cluster-head Robot and other cluster-member Robots assumed to be the optimum distribution for the swarm. While the Robots are moving, they keep measuring the distance between each others by using the Ultrasonic sensor to achieve self-organization within the cluster. Each Robot is programmed to continuously check the distance with cluster-head Robot and also to avoid any obstacle that might be found within the navigation path of the swarm. To view the video clip of this experiment please refer to [57]. Table 6.2 shows the measured distances between the cluster-head (R1) and cluster-members (R2) and (R3) at the final point of each trial, see Figure 6.4-b.

(a) Swarmed Robots Starting from optimum positions

(b) Swarmed Robots at the final navigation point

Figure 6.4: Swarmed Robots navigation: (a) Initial positions, (b) Final positions after navigation

Table 6.2: Distance measurements between Robots starting from optimum positions

No. Trial	R1-R2 distance (cm)	R1-R3 distance (cm)
1	32	27
2	30	22
3	27	29
4	33	20
5	26	19
6	24	30
7	27	18
8	41	27
9	35	20
10	26	24

The *mean* value, usually symbolized as x, can be calculated as the sum of the values divided by their number. This is a sample mean, descriptive of the particular n - times the algorithm was run. Further, the standard deviation can be calculated as:

$$\sigma = \sqrt{\frac{\sum_{i=1}^{n}(x_i - \overline{x})^2}{n}} \tag{6.1}$$

which summarizes the dispersion of values around the mean for that particular sample.

For this experiment, the mean value $\bar{x}_{(R1,R2)}$ and the standard deviation $\sigma_{(R1,R2)}$ for the distances measured between the Robots R1 and R2 are:

$$\begin{aligned} \bar{x}_{(R1,R2)} &= 30.1 \\ \sigma_{(R1,R2)} &= 5.2 \end{aligned}$$

and for the distances measured between the Robots R1 and R3 are:

$$\begin{aligned} \bar{x}_{(R1,R3)} &= 23.6 \\ \sigma_{(R1,R3)} &= 4.4 \end{aligned}$$

6.4.3 Experiment-3: Swarmed Robots starting from random positions

Purpose: Swarmed Robots starting from random positions to reach a pre-specified point after constructing a swarm structure. Swarmed Robots start navigation from random positions to reach a pre-specified point after constructing a swarm structure. This experiment is designed to show the self-organization behaviour for the swarms and how each member in the swarm cooperates with others to achieve a given goal.

Measurements: The convergence of the robots from each other to form a swarm.

Results: The robots should reconstruct a clustered configuration.

This experiment is almost similar to experiment-2 explained above. The difference here is that the Robots starts from random positions within the experiment field. When the cluster-head Robot R1 starts moving forward, the cluster-members R2 and R3 will follow it and start measuring the distance with reference to Robot R1 and makes self adjustment to construct a cluster until they reach the final point of the navigation path. We have measured the distances for 10 trials and it is shown in Table 6.3. Following the same calculations to find out the *mean* value and the *standard deviation* as have been done for experiment-2 in the previous section;

$$\bar{x}_{(R1,R2)} = 29.9$$
$$\sigma_{(R1,R2)} = 5.8$$

and for the distances measured between the Robots R1 and R3 are:

$$\bar{x}_{(R1,R3)} = 28.9$$
$$\sigma_{(R1,R3)} = 8.7$$

It could be observed from the calculations above that the standard deviation is getting higher because the initial positions of the Robots forming a swarm are randomly selected.

Table 6.3: Distance measurements between Robots starting from random positions

No. Trial	R1-R2 distance (cm)	R1-R3 distance (cm)
1	35	40
2	37	39
3	36	33
4	27	35
5	28	29
6	32	27
7	30	19
8	27	13
9	30	32
10	17	22

6.5 Summary

In this Chapter, the hardware implementation for the presented algorithm is explained by using LEGO-NXT Mindstorms Robots. The physical specifications of the robots and communication properties with experimentation are described.

The camera shots in Figure 6.5 shows how the three Robots moves as a unit avoiding any obstacle on the way and keeping the optimum distances between each other. The experiments visual assessment has shown that:

- Each Robot is able to receive messages from the master Robot, within the same local field.
- The Robots can communicate and maintain their positions in order to move as swarm; e.g. the Robot (R1) try to join other two Robots (R2) and (R3) after it has passed the obstacle, Figures 6.5-d and 6.5-e, shows this action respectively.
- Running the experiment with three Robots; R1, R2 and R3, showed that the system provide us with a small real world test bed, because getting the information sent and received within the Bluetooth channels allows us to analyse the Robot's behaviour in the light of real-time responses to; the swarming goals for mobile sensors, avoiding collisions, and moving in clustered base.

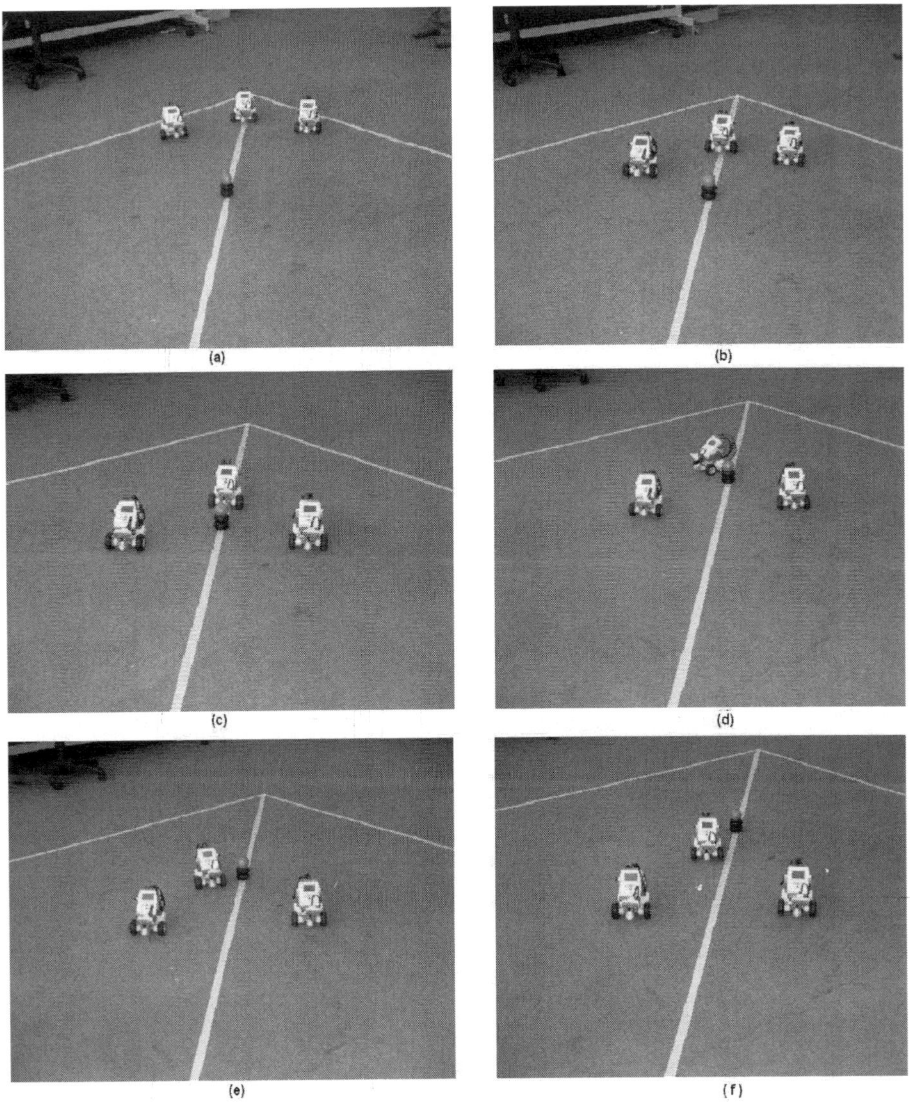

Figure 6.5: Snapshots of swarmed Robots navigation

Chapter 7

Conclusions and Future Work

7.1 Introduction

Wireless Sensor Networks are embedded in the real world and interact closely with the physical environment in which they reside. These networks must be designed to effectively deal with the network's dynamically changing resources, including energy, bandwidth, processing power, node density, and connectivity. Hence, it is important that these sensor networks must be designed to be responsive to such changing conditions while supporting a wide range of traffic demands from the sensor nodes. Traffic demands in sensors networks are different from other traditional networks that have been studied previously because the injected traffic is strongly influenced by, and coupled to, changes in the physical environment that has been instrumented. Furthermore, sensor networks have to deal with the adverse effects from uncertain and dynamic physical environments.

7.2 Research Summary

As a comparison with the previous work, the research in this thesis is presenting an efficient and flexible algorithm for energy optimization of mobile WSNs by dividing the sensor-nodes into clusters to decrease the communication distance and enabling these sensors to move as swarms avoiding unnecessary movements while they are directed to achieve a given goal. The presented algorithm is applicable for both uniform and non-uniform network topologies and suitable for a wide range of WSNs applications, in which the number and the positions of cluster-heads are not predefined. Furthermore, the membership of the sensor-nodes to the cluster-head is related to the shortest distance and it is not necessary that the clusters are uniformly distributed within the network field.

Simulation results show that the presented approach is an efficient and effective method for solving the problem of energy dissipation in mobile WSNs with respect to distance minimization. The ENAMS algorithm was able to find quickly efficient solutions, for example with an 80-node problem, a good solution can be achieved after around 130 generations, as shown in Figure 5.6. This is relatively a high speed to reach the optimum solution with a small number of generations in such optimization problem.

The number of cluster-heads decreases over generations to reach around 25% from the overall number of sensor-nodes in the network as shown in Figure 5.7. This verifies the effectiveness of our algorithm because, as expected, the total distance will be minimized as the number of heads decreases. Our algorithm was able to achieve a distance optimization in an average value of 84% as compared with the required distance when direct transmission is used.

When a single node is near to the sink, that node itself becomes a cluster-head and sends data directly to the sink. Experiments also show that more cluster-heads are needed when a sink is close to the center of a network than when it is located at a network corner. This observation is expected because when the sink is at the center, all regular nodes are located around the sink. As a result, cluster-heads tend to be distributed around the sink. In a densely-deployed region, a middle node is generally elected as cluster-head. Figure 5.2 and Figure 5.3 clearly shows this. No two cluster-heads are near to each other. The GA is likely to merge two nearby cluster-heads into one head to eliminate essentially duplicated communication distances.

Observing the swarm's performance in terms of quality for the average optimum value for the PSO-models; PSO-TVIW and PSO-SSM, it is concluded that PSO-TVIW convergence is slower as compared with PSO-SSM. This is due to constant acceleration coefficients used in PSO-TVIW which affects the rate of convergence.

7.3 Thesis Contributions

This thesis contributes toward the design of a new hybrid optimization algorithm; ENAMS (Energy optimizatioN Algorithm for Mobile Sensor networks) which is based on the Evolutionary Computation and Swarm Intelligence to increase the life time of mobile wireless sensor networks.

- **Evolving the Clustered Sensor Nodes**

The first major contribution of this research is the clustering algorithm (phase-1 of ENAMS algorithm) by using Evolutionary Computations, specifically, Genetic Algorithms (GAs), which is designed to be suitable for large scale mobile wireless sensor networks and provides a robust and energy-efficient communication mechanism by dividing the sensor-nodes into clusters, where the number of clusters is not predefined and the sensors within each cluster are not necessary to be distributed in the same density.

- **Mobile Swarms of Sensors**

The second major contribution of this research is the swarmed clusters of the mobile wireless sensor networks (phase-2 of ENAMS algorithm). This phase of the presented algorithm enables the sensor nodes to move as swarms within the search space while keeping optimum distances by achieving self-organization between the sensor nodes.

- **List of Publications**

Journals:

[1] M. Al-Obaidy, A. Ayesh, and A. Sheta, "Optimizing the communication distance of an ad hoc mobile sensor networks by genetic algorithms," in *Artificial Intelligence Review Journal*, vol. 29, no. 3, pp. 183-194, Springer, 2009.

Doi:10.1007/s10462-009-9148-z

Conferences:

[1] C. Bertelle, M. Al-Obaidy, A. Ayesh, and R. Ghnemat, "Intelligent Land-Use Management and Sustainable Development: From Interacting Wireless Sensors Networks to Spatial Emergence for Decision Making Engineering of Autonomic and Autonomous Systems," in *The Seventh IEEE International Conference and Workshops, IEEE Computer Society, Oxford, England*, pp. 73-78, March 2010.

[2] M. Al-Obaidy and A. Ayesh, "The Implementation of Optimization Algorithm for Energy Efficient Dynamic Ad Hoc Wireless Sensor Networks," in *The 2nd Swarm Intelligence Algorithms Applications Symposium SIASS-09 within the AISB'09 Convention, Edinburgh, Scotland*, April 2009.

[3] M. Al-Obaidy and A. Ayesh, "Optimizing Autonomous Mobile Sensors Network Using PSO Algorithms," in *Proceedings of the International Conference on Computer Engineering and Systems (ICCES'08), Egypt*, November 2008.

[4] M. Al-Obaidy and A. Ayesh, "Energy Efficient PSO-based Algorithm for Optimizing Autonomous Wireless Sensor Network," in *European Simulation and Modelling (ESM'2008) Conference. EUROSIS, Le Havre, France*, October 2008.

[5] M. Al-Obaidy, A. Ayesh, and A. Sheta, "Optimizing the communication distance of an ad hoc mobile sensor networks by genetic algorithms,"

in *Proceedings of the Forth International Workshop on Advanced Computation for Engineering Applications (ACEA08), Jordan*, pp. 17-23, July 2008.

7.4 Future Work

The idea of the presented ENAMS algorithm could be expanded to cover a wider range of mobile Ad hoc wireless sensor networks by considering a hierarchical structure for the sensor nodes where a cluster-head can have a super cluster-head which sends data directly to the sink.

The simulation program could be developed to be suitable for both static and mobile Ad hoc mobile WSNs. Also, more user interaction facilities could be added to the main menu to give the users additional flexibilities for choosing the proper constraints which suits their own inspected algorithms.

The presented ENAMS algorithm could be implemented by using other types of Robots with higher hardware specifications. This will give the possibility of designing more complicated programs that can be fit in the Robot's memory to produce more intelligent and autonomous interactions between the swarms of Robots.

Appendix A

Sample Code for Simulator Design

The code listed below shows the main functions and the important sections of the program used to design the simulator of our proposed ENAMS algorithm.

```
/* crossover function
/* This function performs the crossover between each
/* two consecutive individuals.
/*********************************************************/

int aa[][]=new int [10][8];
for (int i = 0; i < pop.length; i++)
{
  for (int j = 0; j < pop[i].length; j++)
  {
        if (i==ss1)
          {
           System.out.print(pop[i][j]);
       if (j<=3)
           aa[0][j]=pop[i][j];
        else
       aa[1][j]=pop[i][j];
          }
             aa[4][j]=pop[ss1][j];
  }
System.out.println();
}
```

Figure A.1: The Crossover Function

```
/* Mutation function
/* This function mutate two consecutive individuals with a mutation probability
/* to produce a new offspring.
/*****************************************************************/

private void mutation(int pop[][])
{
for(int j=0;j<8;j++)
{
     rand1=(int)(Math.random()*9) ; //to select random cromsome
     rand2=(int)(Math.random()*9) ;
     rand3=(int)(Math.random()*7) ;
     rand4=(int)(Math.random()*7) ;

    // converting the selected bit from 0 to 1
    if (pop[rand1][rand3]==0)
    pop[rand1][rand3]=1;
    else
    pop[rand1][rand3]=0;

    // switching  the selected bit from 1 to 0
    if (pop[rand2][rand4]==1)
    pop[rand2][rand4]=0;
    else
    pop[rand2][rand4]=1;

}

}
```

Figure A.2: The Mutation Function

```
// The following code performs the Selection step of GA algorithm
// this is done by selecting two parents chromosomes from the
// population according to their fitness values.
//*************************************************************/

for (int i=0;i<fit.length;i++)
{
        if (fit[i]>maxa)
        {
            maxa=fit[i];
            ss1=i;
        }
}


System.out.println(":::"+maxd+";"+ss4);
```

Figure A.3: The Selection Function

```
/* distanc function
/* This function is to calculate the distance between any two points
/* in the search space.
/*****************************************************************/

    static  double distanc(int x1,int y1,int x2,int y2)
       {
          return Math.sqrt((double)(x1-x2)*(x1-x2)+(y1-y2)*(y1-y2));
       }
```

Figure A.4: The Distance Function

```
// The following code searchs for the nearest cluster-head position
// for each sensor node.
//****************************************************************/

int[][] moh = new int[h][500];
double mind3[]=new double[h];
      while (qq3<=n1)
     {
         for(int i=0;i<mind3.length;i++)
         mind3[i]=dis(node[qq3][0], node[qq3][1] , chd[i][0], chd[i][1]);

         double min3=mind3[0];
         for(int i=1;i<mind3.length;i++)
         {
              if (mind3[i]<min3)
              {
                   min3=mind3[i];
                   c3=i;
              }
          }
         for (int j=0 ;j<2;j++)
         moh[c3][j]=chd[c3][j];
         moh[c3][b]=node[qq3][0];
         moh[c3][b+1]=node[qq3][1];
         b++;
         qq3++;
     }
```

Figure A.5: The Search Function for Nearest Cluster Head

```
// The following code calculate the fitness value at each generation
// for PSO phase. It is stored in the array "fitness[r]" during each
// iteration of the loop.
//*************************************************************/

int r=0;
double t;

for(int j=0;j<=3;j++)
{
    for (int i=0;i<19;i++)
    {

    fitness[r]=fitness[r]+(dsw[j][i]+(dall[j]/25));

        r++;
    }
}

for (int i=0;i<r;i++)
System.out.println("fit"+fitness[i]);
System.out.println("r="+r);
```

Figure A.6: Sample code to calculate the fitness of PSO

```
// The following code generats the particles of the swarm randomly
// and then calculate the total distance between the cluster-head
// and all cluster-members.
//*************************************************************/

    System.out.println("*** swarm 1 ****");

      for(int i=0;i<swarm_size;i++)
       {
       for(int j=0;j<a1[i].length;j++)
         {
           a1[i][j]=(int)(Math.random()*100);
           dsw[0][i]=dis(a1[0][0],a1[0][1],a1[i][0],a1[i][1]);
         }
       }
           System.out.println();
           dall[0]=dis(0,0,a1[0][0],a1[0][1]);
```

Figure A.7: Sample code to generate the particles of the swarm

```
// The following code shows how the threading technique can be used
// in Java to display the swarms' movement across the search space.
//**************************************************************/

public void run() {
    Thread.currentThread().setPriority(Thread.MIN_PRIORITY);
    while (q1<q){
      q1++;    // infinite loop
      repaint();
     try {
        Thread.sleep(150);
         }
     catch (Exception e) {
       }
                 }
                   }
  public void start() {
    if (kicker == null) {
      kicker = new Thread(this);
      kicker.start();
                            }
                         }
  public void stop() {
    kicker = null;
                         }
static  double dis(int x1,int y1,int x2,int y2)
        {
            return Math.sqrt((double)(x1-x2)*(x1-x2)+(y1-y2)*(y1-y2));
        }
```

Figure A.8: Threading code for displaying Swarm's movement

Appendix B

Robot Programming using NXT-G Graphical Language

B.1 Robot Programming

We have developed our programs for the LEGO-NXT Mindstorms Robots by using the NXT-G graphical programming environment developed by National Instruments for LEGO Robots. Writing an NXT-G program is very much like creating a flowchart. Using a variety of code blocks, you can control motors, introduce delays, play sounds and direct the flow of your code according to the state of sensors and timers, etc.

The main functions which are used in our hardware experimentations are explained in the following sections.

B.1.1 Controller Function

The controller function shown in Figure B.1 below consists of two parts; The first part is used to "initialize" the driving Motors and the second part is the "position loop".

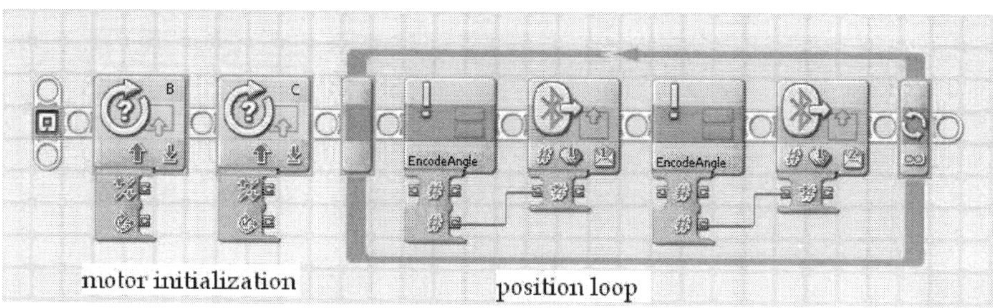

Figure B.1: The Controller Function

B.1.1.1 Motors' initialization

The initialization of the driving motors B and C will effectively makes the starting location for the Robots at the beginning of the program execution to be in the points at which zero velocity will occur.

B.1.1.2 Position Loop

This loop captures the present positions of each motor, encodes the separate sign and magnitude properties into a single signed number and transmits them to separate mailboxes to the receiver module of other Robots.

B.1.2 Encode Angle function

This function uses the direction component (true for forward, false for backward) to determine the appropriate sign of magnitude, and perform the appropriate multiplication (1 for positive or -1 for negative value respectively). This function is shown in Figure B.2.

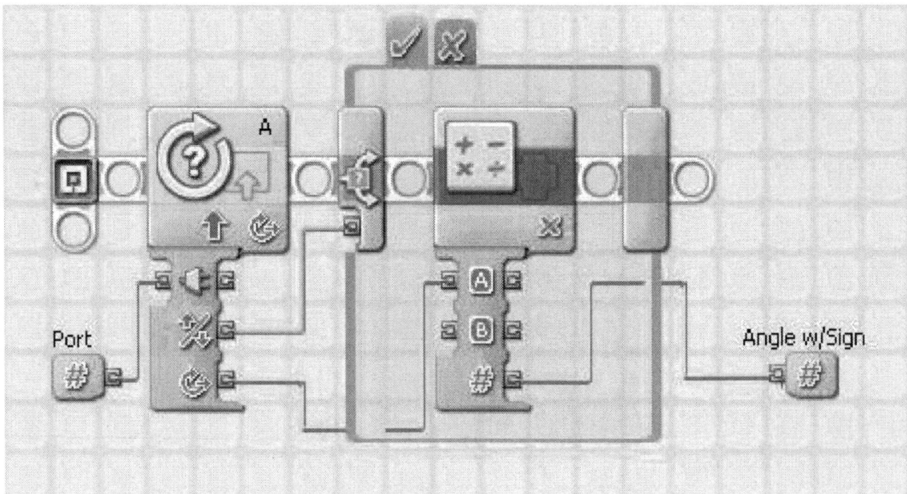

Figure B.2: The Encode Angle Function

B.1.3 Decode Angle function

This function is responsible to decode the angle and speed of the motor movement. It works exactly opposite to the "Encode Angle" function explained above. This function is shown in Figure B.3.

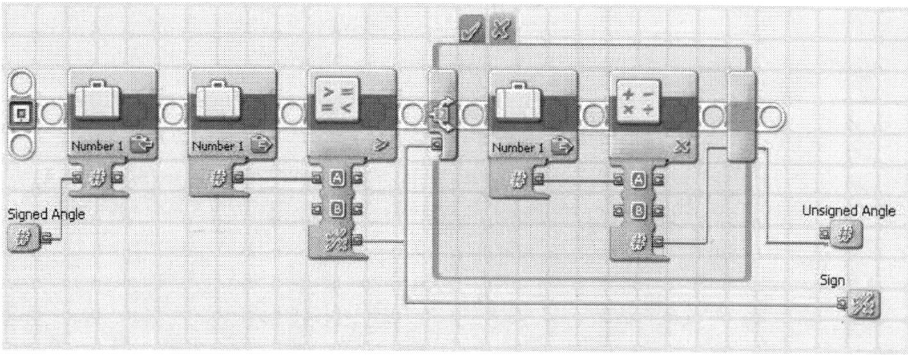

Figure B.3: The Decode Angle Function

B.1.4 Receive function

This function is responsible of capturing the data received through the Bluetooth channel of each Robot. It consists of two parts; the primary thread and the secondary threads as shown in FigureB.4.

The primary thread is responsible for examining the data captured by the Bluetooth receiver module, decomposing these values back into separate sign/magnitude values usable by the motor commands, and mapping the values to the motors.

Each of the secondary threads is responsible for waiting in a loop-state until they detect a message received in the appropriate mailbox. When a message is detected, the inner loop exits and the value received is assigned to the appropriate variable for use by the main thread. The inner loop resumes after the assignment is completed.

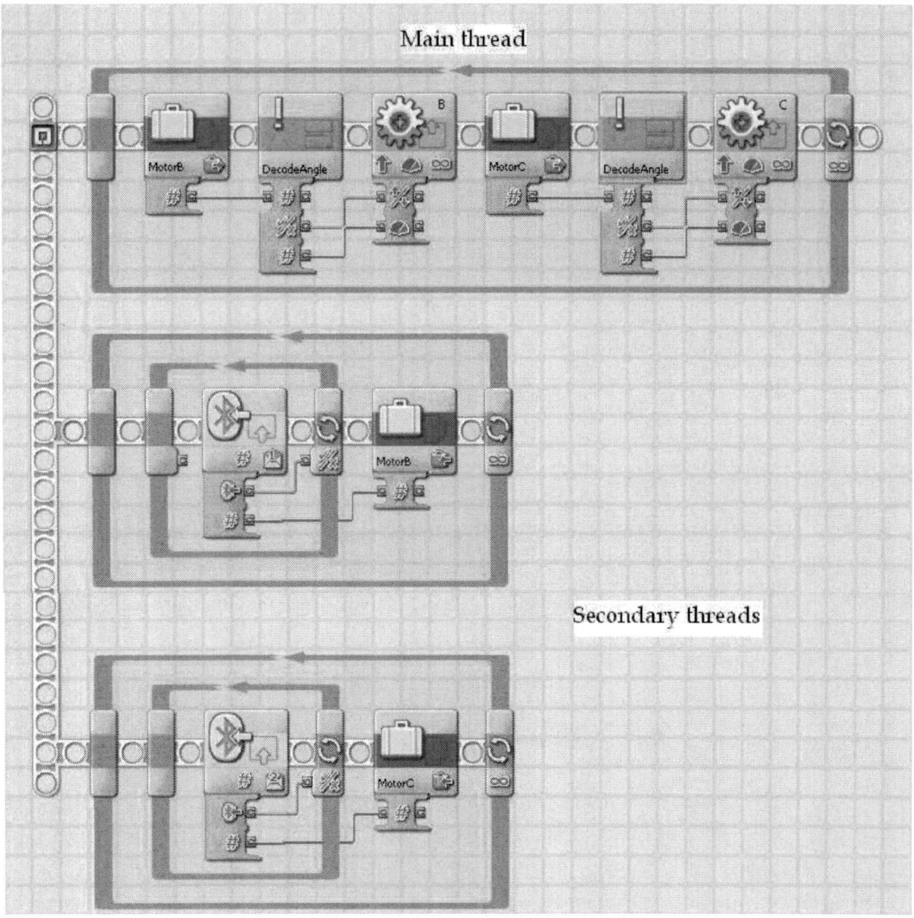

Figure B.4: The Receive Function

References

[1] *DARPA, Network Embedded Systems Technology (NEST): http://dtsn.darpa.mil, Last Accessed: Jan, 2010.*

[2] *http://www.alertsystems.org; Last accessed: January 2010.*

[3] P. Agarwal and C. Procopiuc. Exact and approximation algorithms for clustering. In *Proceedings of the Ninth Annual ACM-SIAM Symposium on Discrete Algorithms*, pages 201–226, California, USA, 1998.

[4] I. Akyildiz, Tommaso Melodia, and K. Chowdhury. A survey on wireless multimedia sensor networks. *Computer Networks*, 51:921–960, 2007.

[5] I. Akyildiz, D. Pompili, and T. Melodia. Challenges for efficient communication in underwater acoustic sensor networks. *ACM Sigbed Review*, 1(2):3–8, 2004.

[6] I. Akyildiz and E.P. Stuntebeck. Wireless underground sensor networks: research challenges. *Ad-Hoc Networks*, 4:669–686, 2006.

[7] I. Akyildiz, W. Su, Y. Sankarasubramaniam, and E. Cayirci. A survey on sensor networks. *IEEE Communications Magazine*, 8(40):102–114, August 2002.

[8] J. Arabas, Z. Michalewicz, and J. Mulawka. Gavps: A genetic algorithm with varying population size. In *Proc. IEEE Int. Conf. on Evolutionary Computation, Orlando*, pages 73–78, Orlando, 1994.

[9] AreaRAE IAQ, RAE Systems. *http://www.raesystems.com; Last accessed: Feb 2010.*

[10] I. Bajec, N. Zimic, and M. Mraz. Simulating flocks on the wing: The fuzzy approach. *Journal of Theoretical Biology*, 233(2):199–220, 2005.

[11] T. Balch and R. Arkin. Communication in reactive multiagent robotic systems. *Journal of Autonomous Robots*, 1(1):1–25, 1994.

[12] S. Bandyopadhyay and E. J. Coyle. An energy efficient hierarchical clustering algorithm for wireless sensor networks. *Proceedings of the IEEE Conference on Computer Communications (INFOCOM)*, 3:1713–1723, 2003.

[13] S. Banerjee and S. Khuller. A clustering scheme for hierarchical control in wireless networks. In *Proceedings of the IEEE INFOCOM2001*, volume 2, pages 1028–1037, Anchorage, Alaska, 2001.

[14] S. Basagni. Distributed clustering for ad hoc networks. In *In Proceedings of the International Symposium on Parallel Architectures, Algorithms and Networks (ISPAN)*, pages 310–315, Washington, DC, USA, 1999. IEEE Computer Society.

[15] Benini, Ernesto, and Andrea Toffolo. Optimal design of horizontal-axis wind turbines using blade-element theory and evolutionary computation. *Journal of Solar Energy Engineering*, 124(4):357–363, November 2002.

[16] F. Bergh and A. Engelbrecht. A cooperative approach to particle swarm optimisation. *IEEE Transactions on Evolutionary Computation*, pages 225– 239, 2004.

[17] C. Bettstetter. *Mobility Modeling, Connectivity, and Adaptive Clustering in Ad Hoc Networks*. PhD thesis, Technische Universitat Munchen, Germany, October 2003.

[18] D. Boeringer and D. Werner. Particle swarm optimization versus genetic algorithms for phased array synthesis. *IEEE Transactions on Antennas and Propagation*, 52:771–779, March 2004.

[19] E. Bonabeau, M. Dorigo, and G. Theraulaz. *Swarm Intelligence: From Natural to Artificial Systems*. NY: Oxford Univ. Press, 1999.

[20] P. Bonnet, J. Gehrke, and P. Seshadri. Querying the physical world. *IEEE Personal Communications*, pages 10–15, October 2000.

[21] F. Bouhafs, M. Merabti, and H. Mokhtar. A semantic clustering routing protocol for wireless sensor networks. In *In Consumer Communications and Networking Conference*, pages 351– 355. IEEE Computer Society, 2006.

[22] Malik Braik, Alaa Sheta, and Aladdin Ayesh. Particle swarm optimisation enhancement approach for improving image quality. *International Journal of Innovative Computing and Applications*, 1(2):138–145, 2007.

[23] M. Carlos, S. Figueiredo, F. Nakamura, and Antonio Loureiro. *Self-Organization Algorithms for Wireless Networks*. Taylor & Francis Group, LLC, 2006.

[24] A. Cerpa, J. Elson, M. Hamilton, and J. Zhao. Habitat monitoring: application driver for wireless communications technology. In *ACM SIGCOMM*, pages 20–41, Costa Rica, April 2001.

[25] H. Chan and A. Perrig. Security and privacy in sensors networks. *IEEE Computer*, 36(10):103–105, Oct 2003.

[26] A. Chandrakasan, R. Amirtharajah, S. Cho, J. Goodman, G. Konduri, J. Kulik, W. Rabiner, and A. Wang. Design considerations for distributed micro-sensor systems. In *Proceedings of the IEEE 1999 Custom Integrated Circuits Conference*, pages 279–286, San Diego, CA, May 1999.

[27] M. Chatterjee, S. Das, and D. Turgut. Wca: A weighted clustering algorithm for mobile ad hoc networks. *Journal of Cluster Computing (Special Issue on Mobile Ad hoc Networks)*, 5:193–204, April 2002.

[28] G. Chen, M.J. Branch, L.Z. Pflug, and B. Szymanski. Sense: A sensor network simulator. *Advances in Pervasive Computing & Networking*, pages 249–267, 2004.

[29] W. Chen, L. Chen, Z. Chen, and S. Tu. Wits: A wireless sensor network for intelligent transportation system. In *First International Multi-Symposiums on Computer and Computational Sciences, IMSCCS '06*, pages 635–641, Hanzhou, Zhejiang, 2006.

[30] S. Cheung, S. Coleri, B. Dundar, S. Ganesh, C. Tan, and P. Varaiya. Traffic measurement and vehicle classification with a single magnetic sensor. *Journal of Transportation Research Board*, 17(19):173–181, December 2005.

[31] Carlos Coello and Maximino Lechuga. Mopso: A proposal for multiple objective particle swarm optimization. In *Proceedings of the Congress on Evolutionary Computation (CEC2002)*, volume 2, pages 1051–1056, Piscataway, NJ, USA, 2002. IEEE Press.

[32] R. Collins and D. Jefferson. Selection in massively parallel genetic algorithms. In *Proceeding of the 4th International Conference on Genetic Algorithms*, pages 249–256, Los Angeles, CA, 1991.

[33] R. Colwell. Hearing on remote sensing as a research and management tool. Technical report, National science foundation, house science committee, September 1998.

[34] O. Cordon, F. Herrera, F. Hoffmann, and L. Magdalena. *Genetic Fuzzy Systems: Evolutionary Tunning and Learning of Fuzzy Knowledge Bases*. World Scientific Publishing Compant Ltd., Singapore, 2001.

[35] O. Cordon, F. Herrera, F. Hoffmann, and L. Magdalena. Ten years of genetic fuzzy sytems: Current framework and new trends. In *Proc. Joint IFSA World Congress and 20th NAFIPS Int. Conf.*, volume 3, pages 1241– 1246, Vancouver, BC, Canada, 25-28 July 2001.

[36] F. Van den Bergh. *An Analysis of Particle Swarm Optimizers*. PhD thesis, Department of Computer Science, University of Pretoria, Pretoria, South Africa, 2002.

[37] M. Dorigo. *Optimization, Learning and Natural Algorithms*. PhD thesis, University of Politecnico, department of Elettronica, Milano, Italy, 1992.

[38] M. Dorigo, G.D. Caro, and L. Gambardella. Ant algorithms for discrete optimization. *Artificial Life*, 5(2):137–172, 1999.

[39] M. Dorigo and Thomas Sttuzle. *Ant Colony Optimization*. MIT press, 2004.

[40] Russell Eberhart and Yuhui Shi. Particle swarm optimization: Developments, applications and resources. In *Proceedings of the 2001 Congress on Evolutionary Computation, CEC2001*, volume 1, pages 81–86, Piscataway, NJ, IEEE Service Center, 2001.

[41] Andries P. Engelbrecht. *Computational Intelligence: an Introduction*. John Wiley & Sons, Ltd, West Sussex, England, 2002.

[42] T. Gao, D. Greenspan, M.Welsh, R. R. Juang, and A. Alm. Vital signs monitoring and patient tracking over a wireless network. In *the 27th Annual International Conference, Engineering in Medicine and Biology Society, IEEE-EMBS' 05*, pages 102–105, Shanghai, September 2005.

[43] M. Gerla, T. Kwon, and G. Pei. On-demand routing in large ad hoc wireless networks with passive clustering. In *In Wireless Communications and Networking Conference (WCNC)*, pages 100–105, Chicago, IL, USA, 2000. IEEE Computer Society.

[44] S.P. Ghoshal. Optimizations of pid gains by particle swarm optimizations in fuzzy based automatic generation control. *Electric Power Systems Research*, 72:203–212, December 2004.

[45] F. Glover. Future paths for integer programming and links to artificial intelligence. *Computers and Operations Research*, 13:533–549, 1986.

[46] F. Glover and G. Kochenberger, editors. *Handbook of MetaHeuristics*. Kluwer Academic Publishers, Boston, MA, 2002.

[47] D. E. Goldberg. *Genetic Algorithms in Search Optimization and Machine Learning*. MA: Addison-Wesley, 1989.

[48] Jinhua Guo, Weidong Xiang, and Shengquan Wang. Reinforce networking theory with opnet simulation. *Journal of Information Technology Education*, 6:215–226, 2007.

[49] N. Hashmi, D. Myung, M. Gaynor, and S. Moulton. A sensor-based, web serviceenabled, emergency medical response system. In *EESR 05: Proceedings of the 2005 workshop on End-to-end, sense-and-respond systems, applications and services*, pages 25–29, Berkeley, CA, USA: USENIX Association, 2005.

[50] A. Hedar, Emad Mabrouk, and Masao Fukushima. Tabu programming method: A new meta-heuristics algorithm using tree data structures for problem solving. Technical report, Department of Applied Mathematics & Physics, Kyoto University, 2008.

[51] J. Heidemann, Y. Li, A. Syed, J. Wills, and W. Ye. Underwater sensor networking: research challenges and potential applications. In *Proceedings of the Technical Report ISI-TR*, pages 603–608, USC/Information Sciences Institute, 2005.

[52] W. Heinzelman and A. Chandrakasan. An application-specific protocol architecture for wireless micro-sensor network. *IEEE Transactions on Wireless Communications*, 1(4):660–670, 2002.

[53] W. Heinzelman, A. Chandrakasan, and H. Balakrishnan. Energy efficient communication protocol for wireless micro-sensor networks. *In Proceedings of the Hawaii International Conference on System Science, Maui, Hawaii*, pages 3005–3014, 2000.

[54] T Hendtlass and Randall. A survey of ant colony and particle swarm meta-heuristics and their application to discrete optimiza-

tion problems. In *Proceedings of The Inaugural Workshop on Artificial Life (AL'01)*, pages 15– 25, Adelaide, Australia, 2001.

[55] F. Heppner and U.Grenander. A stochastic nonlinear model for coordinated bird flocks. In S. Krasner, editor, *Ubiquity of Chaos. AAAS*, Washington, DC, 1990.

[56] A. Hierlemann. Integrated chemical microsensor systems in cmos-technology. In *Proceedings of Solid-State Sensors, Actuators and Microsystems Conference*, volume 2, pages 1134–1137. Digest of Technical Papers, June 2005.

[57] http://www.youtube.com/watch?v=ezc0eUIOZ4Y. *Last accessed: June 2010.*

[58] Xiaohui Hu and Russell Eberthart. Solving constrained nonlinear optimization problems with particle swarm optimization. In *Proceedings of the Sixth World Multiconference on Systemics, Cybernetics and Informatics (SCI2002)*, volume 5, pages 203–206, Orlando, USA, 2002.

[59] Sajid Hussain, W. Matin, and Obidul Islam. Genetic algorithm for energy efficient clusters in wireless sensor network. In *International Conference on Information Technology (ITNG'07)*, pages 147–154, Las Vegas, NV, April 2007. IEEE, Computer Society.

[60] Y. Ichikawa and T. Sawa. Neural network application for direct feedback controllers. *IEEE Trans. Neural Networks*, 3:224–231, Feb. 1992.

[61] T. Imielinski and S. Goel. Dataspace: querying and monitoring deeply networked collections in physical space. In *ACM International Workshop on Data Engineering for Wireless and Mobile Access MobiDE'99*, pages 44–51, Seattle, Washington, 1999.

[62] C. Intanagonwiwat, R. Govindan, and D. Estrin. Directed diffusion: A scalable and robust communication paradigm for sensor networks. *Proc. ACM MobiCom 00, Boston, MA*, pages 56–67, 2000.

[63] C. Ji, Y. Zhang, S. Gao, P. Yuan, and Z. Li. Particle swarm optimization for mobile ad hoc networks clustering. In *IEEE International Conference on Networking, Sensing and Control*, volume 1, pages 372–375, Arizona, USA, 2004.

[64] X. Jiang, J. Polastre, and D. Culler. Perpetual environmentally powered sensor networks. In *4th Int'l Conf. Information Processing in Sensor Networks (IPSN'05)*, Los Angeles, CA, 2005.

[65] Y. Jin, L. Wang, Y. Kim, and X. Yang. Eemc: An energy-efficient multi-level clustering algorithm for large-scale wireless sensor networks. *Computer Networks*, 3(53):542–562, 2008.

[66] K. Jones. Comparision of genetic algorithm and particle swarm optimization. In *International Conference on Computer Systems and Technologies-CompSysTech'2005*, pages IA1–IA8, Bulgaria, 2005.

[67] Chia Feng Juang. A hybrid of genetic algorithm and particle swarm optimization for recurrent network design. *IEEE Transactions on Systems, Man, and CyberneticsPart B: Cybernetics*, 34, No.2:997–1007, April, 2004.

[68] D. Jung and A. Zelinsky. Grounded symbolic communication between heterogeneous cooperating robots. *Journal of Autonomous Robots*, 3(8):269– 292, 2000.

[69] Holger Karl and Andreas Willig. *Protocols and architectures for wireless sensor networks*. John Wiley, 2005.

[70] J. Kennedy and R. C. Eberhart. *Swarm Intelligence*. Morgan Kaufman Publishers, 2001.

[71] J. Kennedy and E. R.C. Particle swarm optimization. *IEEE Inteniational conference on Neural Networks, Perth, Australia*, pages 1942–1948, 1995.

[72] James Kennedy and Russell C. Eberhart. A discrete binary version of the particle swarm algorithm. In *Proceedings of the Conference on Systems, Man, and Cybernetics*, pages 4104–4109, 1997.

[73] R.E. Kenward. Hawks and doves: Factors affecting success and selection in goshawk attacks on woodpigeons. *Journal of Animal Ecology*, 47(2):449– 460, 1978.

[74] Rahul Khanna, Huaping Liu, and Hsiao Chen. Self-organization of sensor networks using genetic algorithms. In *Proceedings of IEEE ICC*, pages 3377–3382, Istanbul, Turky, June 2006.

[75] Rahul Khanna, Huaping Liu, and Hsiao-Hwa Chen. Dynamic optimization of secure mobile sensor networks: A genetic algorithm. In *Proceedings of ICC*, pages 3413–3418, Glassgow, June 2007. IEEE Communications Society.

[76] T. Krink and Lovbjerg. The life cycle model: combining particle swarm optimisation, genetic algorithms and hillclimbers. In *Proceedings of Parallel Problem Solving from Nature (PPSN)*, pages 621–630, Granada, Spain, September 2002.

[77] S. Kumar, Feng Zhao, and D. Shepherd. Collaborative signal and information processing in microsensor networks. *Signal Processing Magazine, IEEE*, 19:13–14, March 2002.

[78] C. Laurent, Didier Helal, Lucille Verbaere, Armin Wellig, and Julien Zory. Wireless sensor networks devices: Overview, issues, state of the art and promising technologies. *ST Journal of Research*, 4(1):8–11, June 2007.

[79] P. Levis, N. Lee, M. Welsh, and D. Culler. Tossim: Accurate and scalable simulation of entire tinyos applications. In *Proc. Int'l Conf. Embedded Networked Sensor Systems (SenSys'03)*, pages 126–137, Los Angeles, CA, November 2003.

[80] D. Li, K. Wong, Y. Hu, and A. Sayeed. Detection, classification, and tracking of targets. *IEEE Signal Processing Magazine*, 19(2):17–29, 2002.

[81] M. Li and Y. Liu. Underground structure monitoring with wireless sensor networks. In *Proceedings of the IPSN*, pages 69–78, Cambridge, MA, 2007.

[82] C. Lin and M. Gerla. Adaptive clustering for mobile wireless networks. *IEEE Journal on Selected Areas in Communications*, 7(15):1265–1275, 1997.

[83] Y. Liu, Z. Qin, and X. He. Supervisor-student model in particle swarm optimization. In *Proceedings of CEC2004 Congress on Evolutionary Computation*, volume 1, pages 542–547, USA, 2004.

[84] R. Marin-Perianu, C. Lombriser, P. Havinga, J. Scholten, and G. Troster. Tandem: A context-aware method for spontaneous clustering of dynamic wireless sensor nodes. In *Proceedings of Internet of Things, the International Conference for Industry and Academia*, pages 342–360. Springer, 2008.

[85] R. Marin-Perianu, J. Scholten, P. Havinga, and P. Hartel. Cluster-based service discovery for heterogeneous wireless sensor networks. *International Journal of Parallel, Emergent and Distributed Systems*, 4(23):325–346, August 2008.

[86] Raluca Marin-Perianu. *Wireless Sensor Networks in Motion Clustering Algorithms for Service Discovery and Provisioning*. PhD thesis, University of Twente, 2008.

[87] A. McDonald and T. Znati. A mobility-based framework for adaptive clustering in wireless ad hoc networks. *IEEE Journal on Selected Areas in Communications (JSAC)*, 8(17):1466–1486, August 1999.

[88] S. Meguerdichian, F. Koushanfar, M. Potkonjak, and M.B. Srivastava. Coverage problems in wireless ad-hoc sensor networks. In *Proceedings of IEEE Infocom conference*, volume 3, pages 1380–1387, Anchorage, AK, USA, April 2001.

[89] MICA2 Wireless Measurement System, Crossbow Technology. *http://www.xbow.com; Last accessed: January 2010.*

[90] Z. Michalewicz. *Genetic Algorithms+Data Structures=Evolution Programs*. New York: Springer-Verlag, 1999.

[91] D. Moriarty and R. Miikkulainen. Efficient reinforcement learning through symbiotic evolution. *Machine Learning*, 22:11–32, 1996.

[92] C. Murthy and B. Manoj. *Ad Hoc Wireless Networks, Architecture and Protocols, pp.191-205*. 2004.

[93] National ICT Australia Ltd. *Castalia - A Simulator for WSNs*, 2009.

[94] The Network Simulator - NS-2. *www.isi.edu/nsnam/ns; Last accessed: May 2008.*

[95] M. Obaidy and A. Ayesh. The implementation of optimization algorithm for energy efficient dynamic ad hoc wireless sensor networks. In *The 2nd Swarm Intelligence Algorithms Applications Symposium SIASS-09 within the AISB09 Convention, Edinburgh, Scotland*, pages 16–22, April 2009.

[96] M. Obaidy and A. Ayesh. Optimizing autonomous mobile sensors network using pso algorithms. In *Proceedings of the International Conference on Computer Engineering & Systems (ICCES'08), Egypt*, pages 199–203, November 2008.

[97] M. Obaidy, A. Ayesh, and A. Sheta. Optimizing the communication distance of an ad hoc wireless sensor networks by genetic algorithms. *Artificial Intelligence Review, Springer*, 29(3):183–194, November 2009.

[98] OPNET network simulator. *http://www.opnet.com; Last accessed: November 2009.*

[99] E.M. Ould-Ahmed-Vall, G.F. Riley, and B.S. Heck. Large-scale sensor networks simulation with gtsnets. *Simulation*, 83:273–290, 2007.

[100] C. Park and P. H. Chou. Ambimax: Autonomous energy harvesting platform for multi-supply wireless sensor nodes. In *Sensor and Ad Hoc Communications and Networks (SECON'06)*, pages 168–177, 2006.

[101] S. Park, A. Savvides, and M.B. Srivastava. Sensorsim: A simulation framework for sensor networks. In *Proc. Int'l Workshop Modeling, Analysis and Simulation of Wireless and Mobile Systems*, pages 104–111, Boston, MA, August 2000.

[102] A. Perrig, J. Stankovic, , and D. Wagner. Security in wireless sensors networks. *Communications of the ACM*, 47(6):53–57, Jun 2004.

[103] E.M. Petriu, N.D. Georganas, D.C. Petriu, D. Makrakis, and V.Z. Groza. Sensor-based information appliances. *IEEE Instrumentation and Measurement Magazine*, pages 31–35, December 2000.

[104] T.J. Pitcher, B.L. Partridge, and C.S. Wardle. A blind fish can school. *Journal of Science*, 194(4268):963–965, 1976.

[105] D. Pompili, T. Melodia, and I. Akyildiz. Deployment analysis in underwater acoustic wireless sensor networks. In *WUWNet*, pages 48–52, Los Angeles, CA, 2006.

[106] G. Pottie and W. Kaiser. Wireless integrated network sensors. *Commun. ACM*, 43, No.50:555–558, May, 2000.

[107] W. Potts. The chorus line hypothesis of manoeuvre coordination in avian flocks. *Journal of Nature*, 309:344–345, 1984.

[108] V. Prasad and S.H. Son. Classification of analysis techniques for wireless sensor networks. In *Proceedings of Int'l Conf. Networked Sensing Systems (INSS'07)*, pages 93–97, Braunschweig, Germany, June 2007.

[109] A. Ratnaweera, S. Halgamuge, and H. Watson. Self-organizing hierarchical particle swarm optimizer with time-varying acceleration coefficients. *Evolutionary Computation, IEEE Transactions*, 8(3):240–255, 2004.

[110] C.W. Reynolds. Flocks, herds and schools: A distributed behavioral model. In *Proceedings of the 14th annual conference on Computer graphics and interactive techniques, SIGGRAPH 87*, pages 25–34, New York, NY, USA, 1987. ACM Press.

[111] J. Robinson, S. Sinton, and Rahmat Samii. Particle swarm, genetic algorithm, and their hybrids: optimization of a profiled corrugated horn antenna. *IEEE International Symposium on Antennas and Propagation. San Antonio, Texas*, June, 2002.

[112] Ayed Salman, Imtiaz Ahmad, and Sabah Al-Madani. Particle swarm optimization for task assignment problem. *Journal of Microprocessors and Microsystems*, 26:363–371, January 2002.

[113] A. Sheta and H. Turabieh. A comparision between genetic algorithms and sequential quadratic programming in solving constrained optimization problems. *ICGST International Jornal on Artificial Intelligence and Machine Learning (AIML)*, 6, No.1:67–74, 2006.

[114] Y. Shi and R. Eberhart. Empirical study of particle swarm optimization. In *Proceedings of the Congress on Evolutionary Computation, CEC 99*, volume 3, pages 1945–1950, Washington, DC, USA, July 1999.

[115] YongLin Shi, DeYuan Gao, Jin Pan, and PuBing Shen. A mobile agent and policy based network management architecture. In *Fifth International Conference on Computational Intelligence and Multimedia Applications (IC-CIMA'03)*, pages 177–181, China, 2003.

[116] E. Shih, S. Cho, N. Ickes, R. Min, A. Sinha, A. Wang, and A. Chandrakasan. Physical layer driven protocol and algorithm design for energy-efficient wireless sensor networks. pages 272–286, Rome, Italy, July 2001.

[117] Jin Shiyuan, Zhou Ming, and Wu Annie. Sensor network optimization using a genetic algorithms. In *7th World Multiconference on Systemics, Cybernetics, and Informatics*, Orlando, Forida, July 2003.

[118] A. Sobeih, J.C. Hou, and L.C. Kung. J-sim: a simulation and emulation environment for wireless sensor networks. *IEEE Wireless Communications*, 13:10–19, August 2006.

[119] K. Soharbi, J. Gao, V. Alawadhi, and G.J. Pottie. Protocols for self-organization of a wirless sensor networks. *IEEE Personal Communications*, 7(5):16–27, 2000.

[120] T. Stathopoulos, D. McLntire, and W. J. Kaiser. The energy endoscope: Real-time detailed energy accounting for wireless sensor nodes. In *Int'l Conf. Information Processing in Sensor Networks (IPSN'08)*, pages 383– 394, St. Louis, MO, 2008.

[121] I. Stojmenovic, M. Seddigh, and J. Zunic. Dominating sets and neighbor elimination-based broadcasting algorithms in wireless networks. *IEEE Transactions on Parallel and Distributed Systems*, 1(13):14–25, 2002.

[122] M. Strohbach and H. Gellersen. Smart clustering - networking smart objects based on their physical relationships. In *Proceedings of the 5th IEEE International Workshop on Networked Appliances*, pages 151– 155. IEEE Computer Society, 2002.

[123] R. Tanese. Distributed genetic algorithm. In *Proceeding of 3rd International Conference on Genetic Algorithms*, pages 434–439, San Francisco, 1989.

[124] Jorge Tavares, J. Fernando Velez, and M. Ferro. Application of wireless sensor networks to automobiles. *Measurement Science Review*, 8(3):65–70, 2008.

[125] D. Thierens. Adaptive mutation rate control schemes in genetic algorithms. In *Proceedings of the IEEE International Conference on Evolutionary Computation*, volume 1, pages 980–985, Honolulu, HI, USA, May 2002.

[126] D. Tian and N. Georganas. A coverage-preserving node scheduling scheme for large wireless sensor networks. In *Proceedings of the 1st ACM international workshop on Wireless sensor networks and applications*, pages 32–41, Atlanta, USA, 2002.

[127] J. Tillett, R. Rao, F. Sahin, and T. Rao. Cluster-head identification in ad hoc sensor networks using particle swarm optimization. In *IEEE International Conference on Personal Wireless Communication*, pages 201–205, NY, USA, 2002.

[128] C. Toh. *Ad Hoc Mobile Wireless Networks Protocols and Systems*. Prentice Hall, 2002.

[129] R. Torah, P. Glynne-Jones, M. Tudor, and S. Beeby. Energy aware wireless micro-system powered by vibration energy harvesting. In *PowerMEMS*, pages 323–326, Freiburg, Germany, 2007.

[130] S. Toumpis and T. Tassiulas. Optimal deployment of large wireless sensor networks. *IEEE Transactions on Information Theory*, 52:2935–2953, 2006.

[131] W. Tsai, C. Ramamoorthy, and O. Nishiguchi. An adaptive hierarchical routing protocol. *IEEE Transactions on Computers*, 8(38):1059–1075, 1989.

[132] S. Tsutsui and D. E. Goldberg. Simplex crossover and linkage identification: Single-stage evolution vs. multi-stage evolution. In *Proceeding of IEEE International Conference, Evolutionary Computation*, pages 974–979, Illinois, USA, 2002. HI.

[133] A. Varga. The omnet++ discrete event simulation system. In *Proc. European Simulation Multiconference*, pages 319–325, Prague, Czech Republic, June 2001.

[134] A. Varga and R. Hornig. An overview of the omnet++ simulation environment. *1st International ICST Conference on Simulation Tools and Techniques for Communications, Networks and Systems*, pages 1–10, May 2008.

[135] Jakob Vesterstrom. Particle swarms - extensions for improved local, multi-modal, and dynamic search in numerical optimization. Master's thesis, Department of Computer Science, University of Aarhus, May 2002.

[136] B. Walker and W. Steffen. An overview of the implications of global change of natural and managed terrestrial ecosystems. *Conservation Ecolog*, 1(2):17–24, 1997.

[137] P. Wan, K. Alzoubi, and O. Frieder. Distributed construction of connected dominating set in wireless ad hoc networks. *Mobile Networks and Applications*, 2(9):141–149, 2004.

[138] C. Wang, K. Sohraby, B. Li, M. Daneshmand, and Y. Hu. A survey of transport protocols for wireless sensor networks. *IEEE Network*, 3(20):34– 40, 2006.

[139] K. Wang, S. Ayyash, T. Little, and P. Basu. Attribute-based clustering for information dissemination in wireless sensor networks. In *Proceedings of the Second Conference on Sensor and Ad Hoc Communications and Networks (SECON)*, pages 498–509. IEEE Computer Society, 2005.

[140] Q. Wang, M. Hempstead, and W. Yang. A realistic power consumption model for wireless sensor network devices. In *Proceedings of IEEE 3rd Annual Communications Society on Sensor and Ad Hoc Communications and Networks (SECON)*, volume 3, pages 286–295, Reston, VA, USA, 2006.

[141] Shamsul Wazed, Ataul Bari, Arunita Jaekel, and Subir Bandyopadhyay. Genetic algorithm based approach for extending the lifetime of two-tiered sensor networks. *2nd International Symposium on Wireless Pervasive Computing ISWPC'07, IEEE*, pages 83–88, 2007.

[142] A. Weddell, N. Harris, and N. White. An efficient indoor photovoltaic power harvesting system for energy-aware wireless sensor nodes. In *Eurosensors'08*, pages 1544–1547, Dresden, Germany, 2008.

[143] Chen Wei-Peng, Hou Jennifer, and C. Lui. Dynamic clustering for acoustic target tracking in wireless sensor networks. *IEEE Transactions on Mobile Computing*, 3:258–271, July/September 2004.

[144] Zhang Wensheng and Cao Guohong. An energy efficient framework for mobile target tracking in sensor networks. *IEEE Proceedings - Military Communications Conference MILCOM, USA*, 1:597–602, 2003.

[145] D. Whitely, S. Dominic, R. Das, and C. W. Anderson. Genetic reinforcement learning for neurocontrol problems. *Mach. Learn*, 13:259–284, 1993.

[146] D. Whitley. Genetic algorithms and neural networks. In M. Galan G. Winter, J. Periaux and P. Cuesta, editors, *Genetic Algorithms Engineering and Computer Science*, pages 191–201. New York: Wiley, 1995.

[147] J. Wu and H. Li. On calculating connected dominating set for efficient routing in ad hoc wireless networks. In *Proceedings of the 3rd international workshop on Discrete algorithms and methods for mobile computing and communications (DIALM)*, pages 7–14, New York, NY, USA, 1999. ACM.

[148] H. Yang and B. Sikdar. A protocol for tracking mobile targets using sensor networks. *Proceedings of the First IEEE workshop on Sensor Network Protocols and Applications*, pages 71–81, May 2006.

[149] J. Yick, G. Pasternack, B. Mukherjee, and D. Ghosal. Placement of network services in sensor networks, self-organization routing and information, integration in wireless sensor networks. *(Special Issue) in International Journal of Wireless and Mobile Computing (IJWMC),* 1:101–112, 2006.

[150] Jennifer Yick, Biswanath Mukherjee, and Dipak Ghosal. Wireless sensor network survey. *Computer Networks,* 52:2292–2330, 2008.

[151] O. Younis and S. Fahmy. Heed: A hybrid, energy-efficient, distributed clustering approach for ad hoc sensor networks. *IEEE Transactions on Mobile Computing,* 4(3):366–379, 2004.

[152] A. Youssef, M. Younis, M. Youssef, and A. Agrawala. Distributed formation of overlapping multi-hop clusters in wireless sensor networks. In *Proceedings of the Global Telecommunications Conference (GLOBECOM),* pages 1–6, 2006.

[153] Bo Zhao and Yi jia Cao. Multiple objective particle swarm optimization technique for economic load dispatch. *Journal of Zhejiang University Science, JZUS,* 6(5):420–427, May 2005.

[154] F. Zhao and L. Guibas. *Wireless Sensor Networks: An Information Processing Approach.* Elsevier Inc., New York, USA, 2004.

[155] Feng Zhao and Leonidas Guibas. *Wireless Sensor Networks: An Information Processing Approach (The Morgan Kaufmann Series in Networking).* Morgan Kaufmann, 2004.

[156] Feng Zhao, Jaewon Shin, and J. Reich. Information-driven dynamic sensor collaboration. *IEEE Signal Processing Magazine,* 9:61–72, March 2002.

INDEX